W Juliet

Volume 4

Story & Art by Emura

W Juliet

Volume 4

Story and Art by Emura

Translation & English Adaptation/William Flanagan
Touch-up Art & Lettering/Mark McMurray
Graphic Design/Hidemi Sahara
Editor/Megan Bates

Managing Editor/Annette Roman
Director of Production/Noboru Watanabe
Vice President of Publishing/Alvin Lu
Sr. Director of Acquisitions/Rika Inouye
Vice President of Sales & Marketing/Liza Coppola
Publisher/Hyoe Narita

Printed in Canada.

Published by VIZ, LLC
P.O. Box 77010
San Francisco, CA 94107
10 9 8 7 6 5 4 3 2 1
First printing, April 2005

www.viz.com

store.viz.com

RATED
T
TEEN
PARENTAL ADVISORY
W JULIET is rated T for Teen. Contains mild sexual situations/humor and tobacco usage. Recommended for ages 13 and up.

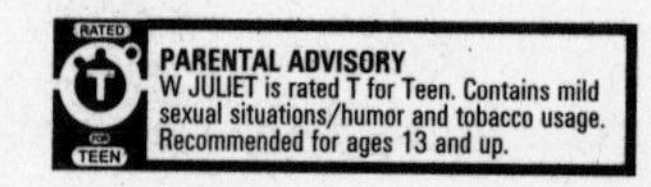

祝
頭!!

W Juliet

-Behind the Scenes Story- ①

I never thought that there would be a page crunch for this story! Even though I had my first front-cover illustration for the magazine! Actually this is where the panel line changed. I worked out the best way through trial and error.

Before → 0.7 Rotring: length 2mm, width 7mm.
After → 0.5 Rotring: length 2mm, width 5mm.

Compare it to Volume 3 and see!

About the school excursion.. My own high school excursion was in Hokkaido. Actually, just before I did these six installments, I went with my sister to Hokkaido.
I talk about the trip in detail (?) in the 1/4-page sections.
You have that to look forward to!

Long ago, I used a 1 cm line.

This panel line is drawn with a 0.1 Rotring.

THE SCHOOL EXCURSION, FOUR NIGHTS AND FIVE DAYS, BEGINS TODAY!
ITO-SAN, WILL YOU BE OKAY ON THE BUS?
I THINK THE SPEED WILL BE OKAY.
BUT IF IT WEAVES BACK AND FORTH ON MOUNTAIN ROADS, THAT'LL BE THE WORST.
I THINK I CAN HANDLE SPEED.
BUT MAKOTO, YOU'D BETTER BE CAREFUL! WE'RE TALKING ABOUT FOUR NIGHTS!
YOU TOO, ITO-SAN! IF YOU FEEL AT ALL UNEASY, COME DIRECTLY TO ME! ♡
DON'T WORRY ABOUT ME! *YOU'RE* THE ONE WITH BIG PROBLEMS, MAKO!
UNDER-STAND? IF YOU NEED ANYTHING...
MI... U... RA!
STMP STMP
I TOLD YOU TO COME IN THE STANDARD GIRLS' UNIFORM!!
HOW MANY TIMES DO I HAVE TO SAY IT?!
TAKE CARE!
...

I THINK WE NEED TO WATCH OUT FOR EACH OTHER.

HELLO EVERYONE! I KNOW YOU'RE ALL TIRED FROM THE FLIGHT...
THE BUS WILL HEAD TO THE TRAPPIST CONVENT.
CHATTER
CHATTER
CHATTER
CHATTER

THE TRAPPIST CONVENT WAS THE FIRST CONVENT FOR FEMALE WORSHIPERS IN JAPAN.
YOU'RE NOT GETTING SICK, MIURA?
NAWW... LET'S SEE... WHERE SHOULD WE TAKE PICTURES WITH MAKO?
ON MY MIDDLE SCHOOL TRIP, I WAS DOWN WITH THE MEASLES.
THIS IS GOING TO BE FUN!!
b-bmp b-bmp
I DIDN'T KNOW YOU GOT MOTION SICKNESS.
SCHEDULE

MAKOTO GETS TO BE WITH US!
EVEN THOUGH WE'RE IN DIFFERENT CLASSES.
THE TWO OF US ARE GOING TO MAKE LOTS OF NICE MEMORIES!
SO *THIS* TRIP...
...I'M GOING TO ENJOY TO THE FULLEST!
KONK

OWW...
AH!
OH, DEAR.
PRINT-OUT
DID I HIT YOU? I'M SOOO SORRY!
BAD CAMERA!
TAKASHI IIZUKA!
...

I ALMOST FORGOT THAT HE'S IN MY CLASS!
HE HASN'T STOOD OUT TOO MUCH RECENTLY.
THAT'S A REALLY IMPRESSIVE CAMERA, IIZUKA!
It's so small!
KYAA
IT'S AMAZINGLY LIGHT!
CHATTER CHATTER
IT WAS MADE ESPECIALLY FOR ME.
IT'S A PROTOTYPE. ONLY ONE IN THE WORLD.

SHALL I PHOTOGRAPH YOU FOR THE "MEMORIES"?
NO THANKS!
heh
I'VE GOT A BAD FEELING ABOUT THIS.
TAKASHI IIZUKA IS THE BROTHER OF TAKAYO, MAKOTO'S FIANCEE IMPOSED BY HIS FATHER.
BOTH BROTHER AND SISTER TRANSFERRED TO SAKURA HIGH TO TRY TO DRAG MAKOTO BACK TO HIS FAMILY.

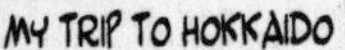

September, 1999. I took some vacation time and went with my sister to Hokkaido. The reason I went? To get material for the manga! We took a three-night, four-day tour. But on the day I was supposed to fly there, my father was driving us to Haneda Airport, and we got stuck in a traffic jam.

She really was mad at me.

Ha ha ha! A manga-ka needs to have a thick skin.

But actually, at the time, there wasn't anything I could do about the situation.. ...so I slept. ♡

Emura doesn't even have a cel phone. She's always at work anyway.

DOOOOOOM
WH--
WHAT IS THIS SUPPOSED TO BE!
MURMUR MURMUR MURMUR
CHATTER CHATTER CHATTER
...
IS THIS FOR REAL?
LOOKS LIKE OUR TOUR BUMPED INTO ANOTHER SCHOOL'S TOUR GROUP.
ALL IN BLACK.
I DON'T WANNA GO IN THERE!
AH! CLASS 3, SO THERE YOU ARE!
!
SORRY! COULD YOU LET ME THROUGH?
MIURA! QUIT PICKING FIGHTS!
I'M NOT!
CHATTER CHATTER
ARRG! I WISH WE WERE IN THE SAME CLASS!
BUMP

OH, NO!
MIURA !!
KYAAA
WHUMPH

...THAT WAS CLOSE.
YOU OKAY?
...
A COMPLETE STRANGER HAS HIS HANDS ALL OVER ME!
SORRY 'BOUT THAT! AND THANKS!
I'M FINE! I'M JUST FINE!
SEE YOU!
ZOOOOM
...
HEY, SAKAMOTO!
WHAT DID YOU GO AND RESCUE A GUY FOR?
I SAW THE WHOLE THING!
IT WOULDA BEEN BETTER IF IT WAS A GIRL!
AH HA HA HA HA HA
YA FOOL!
HA! DIDJA THINK THAT WAS COOL?
CHATTER
CHATTER
CHATTER
OH YEAH! SAKURA HIGH IS A COED SCHOOL.
MUST BE NICE!
LET'S TRY AND GET ONE TO POSE
OKAY!

HIGH SCHOOL STUDENT
STUDENT IDENTITY CARD
THIS IS PROOF THAT THE OWNER OF THIS CARD IS A STUDENT
NATIONAL
NAME
ADDRESS
I DIDN'T KNOW THEY STILL GAVE THESE THINGS OUT.
WEIRD... SHE IS A GIRL.
I LET MY GUARD DOWN!
How embarrassing!
ARE YOU ALL RIGHT, MIURA?
I WAS SURE YOU WERE GOING TO LAND ON YOUR HEAD!
jikk
SHK
HOW COULD I LET MY-SELF GET PAWED LIKE THAT?
YOU... YOU SAW THAT?
WITH ALL THE PEOPLE, WE DIDN'T SEE MUCH.
WHAT HAPPENED WHEN YOU HIT?
B-BMP B-BMP
SHAME
...
THANK GOD MAKO WASN'T HERE!
WHO KNOWS WHAT HE'D SAY?
COME ON! TELL US!
...

KA
CHIK
OKAY, CHEESE!

WE FINALLY GOT OUR PICTURE TAKEN!
WHEE WHEE
WE GET FREE TIME FOR LUNCH!
WHAT'LL WE EAT?
AH!
UMM...
CRAB-RICE, MAYBE?
IT'S DECIDED!
...

DID HE REALLY HAVE HIS HAND ON MY CHEST?
FINALLY, MAKOTO JOINED UP WITH US...
...BUT NOW I HAVE THIS GUILTY CON-SCIENCE...
I SHOULD JUST FORGET IT.
GOTTA HIT THE CAN. I'LL BE RIGHT BACK.
OH!
SLIP
THAK
...
AH!

RRMMMBBL
YO-SHI-RÔ-! WHAT IS THIS ALL ABOUT?!
YOU THINK THIS MAKES YOU COOL?
SORRY! JUST FORGET IT, OKAY?
I HEARD THAT THEY FOUND CIGARETTES ON A STUDENT LAST YEAR, AND THEY FORCED HIM TO GO HOME EARLY!
YOU IDIOT!
HEY! HURRY UP AND THROW THEM OUT!
YOU STUDENTS OVER THERE!
BYOING
YOU KNOW THE MEET-UP TIME?
SURE! WE HAVE 50 MINUTES, RIGHT?
DON'T BE LATE!
HAND OFF!
KYAA!
I DON'T WANT 'EM!
!
THUMP
MAKE SURE YOU'RE ON TIME!
OKAY !!
TMP TMP
LUNCH WAS GREAT!
NICE SHOT...
THEY FELL RIGHT IN MY BAG.
EH?

GIVE IT TO ME. I'LL THROW THEM OUT.
I DON'T SEE ANY TRASH CANS AROUND.
AND THE TEACHERS ARE ALL IN THE SMOKING SECTION.
↑ Where the trash can is.
喫煙
THEN I'LL KEEP THEM.
WHAP
WHAT FOOL WOULD GIVE DANGEROUS THINGS LIKE THOSE TO YOU?!
IT'S ALL RIGHT. I WON'T SCREW UP.
I'LL TOSS THEM AS SOON AS I GET A CHANCE.
LET'S GO.
NOT THAT WE'VE GOT ANYPLACE SPECIAL TO GO.
...
SHHHH
SPLISH SPLISH
MAKOTO'S IN MORE DANGER THAN I AM.
WE'RE FINALLY ON A TRIP TOGETHER AND NOW...
I'M GONNA KILL YO-SHIRÔ!
squee
BUT...
...THAT ISN'T THE ONLY PROBLEM...
FLIP

A PIC-TURE?
PAK
IT'S FROM THIS MORNING!!
THIS--
THIS IS...
A NICE CAMERA ANGLE, DON'T YOU THINK?
!!
TAKASHI IIZUKA !!
Y-YOU...
WHEN DID YOU TAKE THIS?
THE MOMENT I SAW YOU IN THE BEST POSITION FOR A PHOTO-GRAPH.
IF YOU DON'T WANT MAKOTO-KUN TO SEE IT, I SUGGEST YOU BREAK OFF RELATIONS.
I KNEW THAT WAS COMING!
FOR THIS LITTLE THING?
GANCH
IT MAY BE LITTLE...

BUT QUANTITY INCREASES ITS IMPORTANCE.
FWOOSH
WAAA!!!

WHAT?
HUH? A PHOTO?
CHATTER
GLIP GLIP GLIP GLIP GLIP GLIP
WHOOSH

WONDERFUL!
KLAP KLAP KLAP KLAP
pant wheeze
...
I HAVE THE NEGATIVES.
IF YOU DON'T DO AS I SAY, THE WORLD WILL SEE THEM.
THAT WAS SO LOW!!
WHSH
I'M AFRAID YOU'RE IN THE WAY.
DO YOU ENJOY DISAPPOINTING HIM LIKE THIS?

...!!
YOU GOTTA BE KIDDING! I'LL NEVER BE THAT JERK'S PUPPET!
I HAVE TO GET THOSE NEGATIVES BACK!
glance glance glance glance
ITO-SAN, WAS THE RESTROOM CROWDED?
WHAT'S WRONG?
OH, NOTHING!
GOOD! HE ISN'T HERE!
BUT WHAT'LL I DO?
I HAVE TO TELL MAKO BEFORE HE TAKES IT THE WRONG WAY!
b-bmp b-bmp
BUT IT DOESN'T SEEM NATURAL TO BRING IT UP.
TO JUST BLURT IT OUT...
b-bmp b-bmp
b-bmp b-bmp

...THE GIRLS I'M ROOMING WITH WILL BE VISITING THE PEOPLE NEXT DOOR.
I'LL BE ALONE FOR TWO OR THREE HOURS.
TO-NIGHT...

COME KEEP ME COMPANY, ITO-SAN.
!

YOU DON'T MIND?
I *WANT* YOU WITH ME!
PROMISE?

ALL RIGHT!
b-bmp b-bmp
b-bmp b-bmp

FWOOGH
GA?

...
GLIP GLIP GLIP GLIP GLIP GLIP

...

SORRY, MAKO...
SHP
...I'VE GOT SOMETHING I HAVE TO DO.

BUT I'LL KEEP MY PROMISE!
SEE YOU LATER!
TMP
?!
HOLD IT!!

IT'S AN IIZUKA BODY-GUARD!
THE NEGATIVES!
HOLD IT RIGHT THERE!!
HYUUM
IT LOOKS LIKE THE GAME OF TAG HAS BEGUN.
!
I'M JUST TEASING HER A LITTLE.
PHWIT
WHAT ARE YOU PUTTING HER THROUGH THIS TIME?
HEH
IT'S JUST A PICTURE I TOOK.
SIGH
SHE'S AFTER THE NEGA-TIVES.
IT'S SOMETHING SHE REALLY DOESN'T WANT YOU TO SEE.

IT'S A KISS...
...WITH SOME UNKNOWN MAN.
DAMMIT! WHY?
I CAN'T WASTE A DAY THIS IMPOR-TANT!
WILL YOU JUST...
...STOP ?!!
FWAK
!
DOMP
I DID IT!
TRMP
TMP TMP
WHUMP
I ALMOST CAUGHT HIM!
...
OW...

GRAB
!!
...OWCH.
GLINT
AHA!
I HAVE THE NEGATIVES!!
RRIPP
!
JUST WHAT DID YOU HOPE MY REACTION WOULD BE?

YOU'RE LOOKING RATHER PALE.
I FEEL SORRY FOR HER.
SHE CONSTANTLY STAYS BESIDE YOU, PROTECTING YOU...
...WITH-OUT ANY REWARD UNTIL YOU GRADUATE.
IF THE TRUTH IS DISCOVERED, EVERYTHING WILL POP LIKE A SOAP BUBBLE.
BECAUSE YOU ALREADY HAVE A FINE FIANCEE NAMED TAKAYO.
...
AND IN THE END, WHEN YOU RETURN TO YOUR DUTIES AND YOUR FAMILY, ITO WILL HAVE BEEN A SHORT DALLIANCE.
PERHAPS YOU SHOULD BECOME MORE SERIOUS ABOUT YOUR FUTURE.
POFF
STOP LIVING IN DREAMS.
GRABB
WH--
...
PAT

ALL THE CLASSES ARE MEETING UP. YOU'LL BE LATE.
BE CAREFUL, WON'T YOU?
GRIN
HA!
I'VE WON!
MAKOTO-SAN!
THEY'RE LOADING THE CLASS 3 BUS!
CHATTER
CHATTER
CHATTER
CHATTER
TIME SURE FLIES, HUH?
CHATTER
CHATTER
HEY, WHAT DID YOU DO...
...WITH THE CIGARETTES?
OH...
I FOUND A TRASH BAG TO PUT THEM IN.
GRIN
WHAT'S THAT?
NOTHING.
CHATTER
CHATTER
I'M GLAD! IT COULD HAVE BEEN THE WHOLE DAY...
...BUT THEY ONLY RAN ME AROUND FOR HALF A DAY.
CRUNCH
KASHUNK
EXCUSE MY TARDINESS.
OH, IIZUKA. YOU'RE THE LAST.

NEXT TIME, BE EARLIER.
BUMP
YES, SIR...
HEY, WAIT A MINUTE!
LET'S SEE WHAT YOU HAVE IN YOUR POCKET!
EH?
OH, COME ON. YOU MEAN THIS?
IT'S JUST MY CAMERA.
SEE?
SWIKK

GRRRRR
MMMM
YOU LITTLE...
...YOU'VE GOT SOME NERVE!
EH?
?!!
THAT TAKES GUTS!
CHATTER CHATTER
"BE CAREFUL, WON'T YOU?"
THAT CRETIN !!
THEY AREN'T MINE!!
YOU CAN TELL ME ALL ABOUT IT AT THE HOTEL.

AH HA HA HA HA HA HA!!
IT WAS YOU, MAKOTO-SAN, WHO PLANTED THE CIGARETTES?
I'LL BET THEY'RE GOING TO SEND HIM HOME NOW!
YOU SWITCHED THEM FOR THE CAMERA?
CLASS 5 WAS BUZZING ABOUT IT!
HA HA
HA HA
HE'S ALWAYS TRYING TO GET OTHER PEOPLE IN TROUBLE!
HA HA HA!
YEAH, I HEARD THAT TOO!
...
I WONDER WHAT THEY ACTUALLY TALKED ABOUT.
COULD IT BE...
SSIP
OKAY... HOLD DOWN THE FORT, MAKOTO-SAN!
SHHT
YOU HAVE FUN TOO, ITO-SAN!
SHHT
KACHAK
...
SLIP

NOW...
!!
HE'S QUICK!
MAKO! ISN'T THAT RECKLESS? ANYBODY COULD COME BY...
THE DOOR LOCKS AUTO-MATICALLY. WE'RE FINE.
WE'RE FINALLY ALONE!
grin
LET'S GO OUT ON THE VERANDA...
THERE'S A NICE VIEW.
I DON'T KNOW IF I'M EMBAR-RASSED OR HAPPY!
DID YOU MANAGE TO GET THE NEGATIVES BACK?
YUKATA ARE PRETTY SEXY.
YEAH, I EVENTUALLY GOT THEM.
...
BLUUUUUSH
I KNOW ABOUT THE PHOTO.
TAKASHI-SAN SHOWED ME.

IT WAS A PRETTY IMPRESSIVE KISS SCENE.
heh
EYAAAAHH!!
NO! I'M SORRY! BUT IT WASN'T THAT!
HE CAUGHT ME WHEN I FELL!!
IT MAY HAVE LOOKED THAT WAY IN THE PICTURE BUT...
heh
...IT NEVER HAP-PENED!
I KNOW THAT!
ONE LITTLE PICTURE ISN'T ENOUGH TO MAKE ME DOUBT YOU.
...!
THE WORDS TAKASHI USED WITH ME WERE MORE EFFECTIVE THAN THE PICTURE.
?
HUH?
THAT YOU, ITO-SAN, ARE JUST A DALLIANCE FOR ME.
IF YOU THINK ABOUT IT, IT COULD BE SEEN THAT WAY.

YOU'VE BEEN DRAGGED INTO MY SITU-ATION...
IT'S CON-STANTLY CREATING TROUBLE FOR YOU.
SINCE I'M IN WOMEN'S CLOTHES, I CAN'T PROTECT YOU LIKE A MAN!
I'M PRETTY AWFUL!
NOW WAIT! I'VE NEVER THOUGHT THAT FOR A SECOND!
I'M HELPING YOU BECAUSE I WANT TO!
IT'S A SICK-NESS!
...
LET'S BREAK FATHER'S RULES AND RUN OFF TO ELOPE!
!
BLUSSH
YOU IDIOT! HOW CAN YOU SAY SOMETHING SO SILLY?
DON'T GO WEAK ON ME!
WHAPP
SORRY, SORRY. IT WAS JUST A PLAN B.
DON'T WASTE ALL THE HELP I'VE GIVEN YOU!

BUT IF MY SECRET GOT OUT, I MIGHT RUN SOMEWHERE AND DRAG YOU ALONG WITH ME.
OH, IS THAT SO?!
...
I'M PREPARED TO DO IT.
REMEMBER THAT.
"PLAN B"...
FINE.
I'LL GO WITH YOU, BUT...

ITO...
JUST IN CASE, FOR PLAN B!!
YOU MUST NEVER GIVE UP ON YOUR DREAM!!
IF YOU DO, I'M NOT GOING ANYWHERE WITH YOU!
THAT'S MY VOW...
...TO NEVER GIVE UP.
...

AH!

WHAT'S THAT? THAT GUY YOU SAVED TODAY?
SHE WAS A GIRL.
Chatter
Chatter
DID YOU STEAL THAT?
IT WAS A GUY! ARE YOU BLIND?
YOU'RE THE ONE WHO'S BLIND. SEE?
WHAT?!
I JUST GOT SAKURA HIGH'S ENTIRE SCHEDULE FOR THE TRIP!
SCHEDULE
WHOA!!
HEY! OUR FREE DAYS ARE THE SAME!
I KNEW IT!
THEY HAVE A LOT OF CUTE GIRLS, RIGHT?
HIGH-CLASS BROADS!
YAY
YAY
...
KANAGAWA PREFECTURE PUBLIC SCHOOL, SAKURA-GA-OKA HIGH SCHOOL...
ITO MIURA.
THIS IS PROOF THAT THE OWNER OF THIS
NATIONAL
NAME ITO MIURA
ADDRESS
VALID UNTIL XX/XX/20XX
KANAGAWA PREFECTURE
PUBLIC SCHOOLS
SAKURA-GA-OKA HIGH SCHOOL
I HOPE I SEE YOU AGAIN.

熊出没注意

CURFEW IS AT 6:30.
MAKE SURE YOU LEAVE YOUR KEYS AT THE DESK.

IF ANYTHING UNUSUAL HAPPENS, CONTACT THE HOTEL.
Chatter chatter
OKAY!
I WANT YOU ALL TO ACT LIKE RESPONSIBLE STUDENTS.
Chatter chatter
DIS-MISSED!
TRY NOT TO GET INTO ANY TROUBLE, AND TRAVEL IN GROUPS!
THIRD DAY OF THE SCHOOL EXCURSION.
THE LONG-AWAITED FREE DAY.
BUT...

-Behind the Scenes Story- 2
Sapporo streets are so convenient! It's impossible to get lost! And I have no sense of direction!
WHAT DO YOU SEE AROUND YOU?
I DON'T REALLY KNOW.
WHY DO I GET SO LOST?
WHERE ARE YOU?
←I always drove my previous editor crazy! I could never make it to the editorial offices!
A BANK...
It happened a bunch of times!
I admit it! I'm just the worst when it comes to going to a new store.
IT'S EASY TO FIND THE KANDA BOOKSTORES. JUST GO OUT FROM THE SUBWAY AND WALK STRAIGHT AHEAD.
IT'S RIGHT THERE.
Previous editor, Mr. E. Kawa.
OKAY!
E
Subway
This way. →
THE WRONG WAY!
My problem happened before my editor's directions. After wandering around for an hour, I realized I was in the wrong place.

...
LOOK OVER THERE!
WHAT SCHOOL IS SHE FROM?
IS SHE A MODEL?
LOOK AT THOSE INCREDIBLE LEGS!
STARE
STARE
STARE
STARE
STARE
STARE
I KNEW I SHOULD NEVER HAVE WORN MY UNIFORM!
NOW EVERYBODY'S STARING!
GLOOM
ITO-SAN!
I BOUGHT US SOME CORN ON THE COB.
I WANT TO CHANGE CLOTHES!
MUNCHA MUNCHA
DON'T BE THAT WAY. ♪
YOU WANTED TO TRY IT, RIGHT?
THEY'RE STARING IN ADMIRATION.
YOU'RE HAVING FUN, AREN'T YOU?
DON'T WORRY! YOU LOOK CUTE IN A SKIRT! ♡
IT ALL HAPPENED ONE HOUR EARLIER.

IT STARTED WITH SOMETHING I SAID TO MAKOTO.
EH?
A UNIFORM?
YEAH! I'VE NEVER SEEN YOU IN A GUY'S UNIFORM BEFORE!
NOW'S YOUR BEST CHANCE! TRY IT!
WE HAD INDIVIDUAL ROOMS IN LAST NIGHT'S HOTEL, SO WE WERE SAFE.
YOU'RE PERFECT FOR THE PART!
LIKE A PUNK.
THEY CAN COME AND GO AS THEY LIKE.
AH HA HA HA!
AND WE JOKED ABOUT THINGS LIKE THIS.
IF ONLY IT WERE A JOKE!
WELL I HAVEN'T SEEN YOU IN A SCHOOL UNIFORM EITHER, ITO-SAN.
AFTER ALL, FAIR IS FAIR.
AFTER THAT...
...THINGS WENT THE WAY THEY WENT.

THE "JOKE" STARTED THEN AND KEPT ON GOING.
IS IT OKAY FOR YOU TO WALK AROUND DRESSED THAT WAY?
IT'S FINE! EVERYBODY'S SPREAD THROUGHOUT THE CITY!
AND THERE ARE A LOT OF STUDENTS FROM OTHER SCHOOLS AROUND.
EVEN IF WE MET PEOPLE WE KNOW, THEY WOULDN'T RECOGNIZE US.
YOU'VE BEEN GETTING TOO RECKLESS LATELY!
grin
I WANTED TO BE ABLE TO WALK WITH YOU THIS WAY AT LEAST ONCE.
!
I WANTED TO TRY IT. US LOOKING NORMAL, YOU IN YOUR UNIFORM...
WELL...
EVEN IF TODAY IS THE ONLY DAY WE CAN EVER DO IT.
...
IN THE END...
I GUESS...
...THAT I CAN PUT UP WITH IT...
...FOR ONLY ONE DAY.
THUMP

I CAN NEVER REFUSE MAKOTO.
CRYSTAL-KAN
WOW !!
WHAT IS THIS? ARE THESE THINGS REALLY MADE BY HAND?
THAT'S COOL !!
A GLASS BOAT, HUH?
MY BIG BROTHER YÛTO WOULD LOVE THIS!
CLEVER
HOW MUCH?
B-BMP
B-BMP
... ...
I FOUND ONE! A SOY-SAUCE COASTER!
...
500 yen
50,000 yen
!
chatter
chatter
PRESENTS FOR THE FAMILY...
THE PROBLEM WITH GLASS IS IT'LL PROBABLY BREAK.
chatter
chatter
glance
glance
WHAT TO GET...?

I didn't have a source for this drawing.

sst
BUMP
chatter chatter
AH!
EX-CUSE ME.
!!
SHKK
DAMMIT!
KYAA! THANK YOU FOR SHOPPING WITH US!
chatter
chatter
chatter
chatter

AHH!
ITO-SAN...?
WHAT IS THIS?! I HAVEN'T SEEN A SINGLE SAKURA HIGH GIRL!
THIS PLACE BLOWS!
MAYBE IN SAPPORO?
BUT THERE ARE PLENTY OF GIRLS IN SAILOR SUITS.
YEAH!
chatter chatter
KRASSH
RATTL
RATTL
WHAT'S ALL THE NOISE?
BUMP
OW!
HOLD IT, YOU LITTLE JERKS!
THWAK
AAH!

WHAT'S WITH THAT GIRL?
chatter
SHE'S A TALL ONE!
!
GIMME BACK MY MONEY!
WHOOSH
EYAAH!
LOOK AT THAT!!
THAT GIRL JUST OVER-POWERED HIM!
SHE'S GOOD!
...
CATCH!
GRIMP
HEY!
KAKK
DAMMIT! THERE'S TWO OF 'EM!
JEEZ!
DAMN LOCAL KIDS!

heh
I DON'T THINK YOU SHOULD BE SO COCKY!
AAAAAH!!
HERE'S YOUR WALLET.
YOU'VE GOT COURAGE, DON'T YOU?
grin
TMP TMP
AHHHHH!! YOU'RE THE GUY FROM THE CONVENT!!
185 cm (6'1")
RIGHT! I CAME TO YOUR RESCUE.
NICE TO SEE YOU AGAIN, MIURA-CHAN!
MIURA-CHAN?!?
AND HOW'D YOU KNOW MY NAME?
SO YOU'RE WEARING YOUR PROPER UNIFORM THIS TIME.
I DIDN'T RECOG-NIZE YOU AT FIRST.
REALLY?!
YOU CHANGED INTO A GIRL.

WE WERE FATED TO MEET, HUH?
...
shake shake
HIS SELF-CONFIDENCE...
...IT REMINDS ME OF SOMEBODY.
I WONDER WHO?
IT SEEMED...
...AT THE TIME, HE WAS A COOL, SERIOUS GUY.
grin
?
HERE.
FLIP

!
MY SCHOOL I.D. CARD!
RIGHT. I FOUND IT WHERE YOU FELL.
IT'S KIND OF RISKY LOSING YOUR I.D. WHEN YOU'RE ON A TRIP.

I DIDN'T REALIZE!
SST
AND...
AS A THANK YOU FOR ALL OF THIS...

FINALLY ARRIVING AT HANEDA AIRPORT

We just barely made it!

ONLY FIVE MINUTES TO GO!

UM... LET'S SEE...

SO WHERE'S THE GATE?

One end — Over 200 meters away! — Here

Present location — In the farthest end

...

I never expected us to do something so much like a manga! While we were running we heard our names being called.

WILL THE EMURA PARTY... ...REPORT IMMEDIATELY TO...

DASH

AHHH! THAT'S US!

We ran full out for the first time in a long time, but somehow we managed to make it to the gate without incident. And I flew on a plane for the very first time!

• It was the second time for my sister.

Actually, my high school did the same thing and took its school excursion to Hokkaido. But my class had to take the bullet train. My sister was able to go by airline. Dammit!!

...SPEND THE REST OF THE DAY WITH ME.

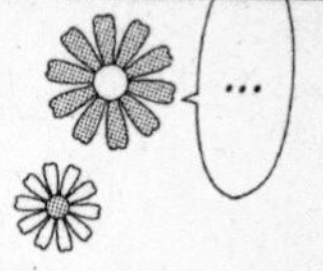
...

HUH?

I DON'T HAVE ANY INTEREST IN ORDINARY GIRLS.

?!
IT COULD BE YOUR COURAGE, IT COULD BE THE LOOK IN YOUR EYES, BUT I'VE TAKEN A LIKING TO YOU!
GRIN
AND IT DOESN'T HURT THAT YOU'RE PRETTY HOT.
SEE... I'M FROM A BOYS' SCHOOL.
AND IF I CAN BE SEEN WALKING WITH A GIRL, IT'LL BOOST MY REPUTATION.
IT'S A GUY'S DREAM, RIGHT?
HELP ME OUT FOR A BIT?
SOMEHOW...
...I UNDERSTOOD THAT HE WAS...

...JUST LIKE TOKI-CHAN!!
SAKAMOTO...
HIS DROOPY EYES AND ATTITUDE...

YOU KNOW THAT GIRL?
YEAH, SHE'S MY GIRLFRIEND!
Ito.

FOR THIS ONE DAY YOU ARE, RIGHT?
WHOOSSHH
I AM NOT!
IT'S TROUBLE FOR YOU IF YOU DON'T HAVE THIS.
PLIK
AH!
GIVE IT BACK, YA JERK!!
AHHAHAHAHAHA
THEY'RE IN LOVE, HUH?
I WISH IT WAS ME.

Played into Sakamoto's hands.

I WANT TO GO BACK TO MAKOTO!
I DON'T HAVE TIME TO DO THIS STUFF!
huff huff
HE'S TOO FAST!
LET ME BORROW YOUR GIRL!
FIND YOUR OWN!
I ENVY YOU! SECOND SEMESTER YOU GET TO ESCAPE THE ALL-MALE HELL!
BUT IT'S GOTTA BE ROUGH TRANSFER-RING TO A NEW SCHOOL.
WHAT CHOICE DO I GOT? THEY MOVED MY DAD'S JOB.
IS IT A COED SCHOOL NEXT?

UHHHH...
MY FAMILY ALWAYS MOVES AROUND, BUT THE SCHOOLS ARE THE SAME.
MAINLY BECAUSE MY DAD WENT TO A BOYS' SCHOOL.
NO...
...IT'LL PROBABLY BE A GUYS' SCHOOL.
AND SINCE I'M THE ELDEST SON...
...I'M PRETTY MUCH RESIGNED TO HIM RUNNING MY LIFE.
...
CRYSTAL-KAN
EXCUSE ME. I'M LOOKING FOR SOMEONE.
I DON'T KNOW... GUYS ALL LOOK ALIKE TO ME THESE DAYS...
UM... TODAY SHE'S WEARING THE SAME UNIFORM AS THE ONE ON THE RIGHT.
EH?! THAT'S A GIRL?!
...

SORRY, BUDDY! I DIDN'T KNOW!
HA HA HA
I GUESS THIS PICTURE JUST WON'T HELP.
I GET THAT REACTION TOO MANY TIMES.
I ONLY TOOK MY EYES OFF HER FOR A SECOND!
I JUST HOPE SHE ISN'T INVOLVED IN ANYTHING WEIRD.
EHHHH ?!
SAKAMOTO'S WITH A SAKURA HIGH GIRL?
CHATTER
HOW'D THAT HAPPEN?
DAMMIT! HE'S SO LUCKY!
HEY! WOW!
IT'S NO FAIR! HE ALWAYS GETS THE GOOD STUFF!
AND SHE'S A CLASSY ONE, TOO! REMEMBER? THE ONE FROM THE I.D.
THAT WAS A GIRL ?!
OH, YOU MEAN... WHAT WAS HER NAME... ITO MIURA!
HE SAID HE WANTED HER TO BE HIS GIRLFRIEND FOR THE DAY AND WENT OFF WITH HER!
THE GUY CAN BE PRETTY IMPOSING.
SO WHERE'RE THEY GOING? BACK TO SAPPORO?
HE SAID SOMETHING ABOUT ÔDORI PARK...
13 16
National

WHY...
...DO I...
...HAVE TO SPEND MY PRECIOUS TIME...
...HANGING AROUND WITH THIS GUY?!
ラーメン
みそラーメン
SLUMP
DON'T YOU WANNA EAT? YOUR RAMEN'S GETTING COLD.
BAM
I TOLD YOU...
YOU DON'T NEED TO PARADE ME THROUGH OTARU ANYMORE!
WHY DON'T YOU TAKE ME BACK TO SAPPORO STATION AND GET GONE!
SSSSSIP
...
Sapporo is quite a ways from Otaru.
HUFF HUFF
TUMP
I GET IT! WHAT YOU WANT...
...IS TO WALK WITH ME AROUND SAPPORO! ♡
HE DOESN'T GET IT! HE DOESN'T!
THINK NORMAL FOR JUST A SECOND, WILL YOU?
OH, DON'T BE THAT WAY!
YOU CAN SPEND A LITTLE TIME WITH ME!

LOOK! A TV BROADCAST TOWER!
I'M EX-HAUSTED.
I'M GOING TO SLEEP.
I WAS ALREADY HERE THIS MORNING.
MAKOTO...

HE'LL BE MAD AT ME AGAIN.
I WONDER IF HE'S LOOKING FOR ME.

IN REALITY, HE WAS THE ONE...
...I WAS SUPPOSED TO SEE THE SIGHTS WITH.

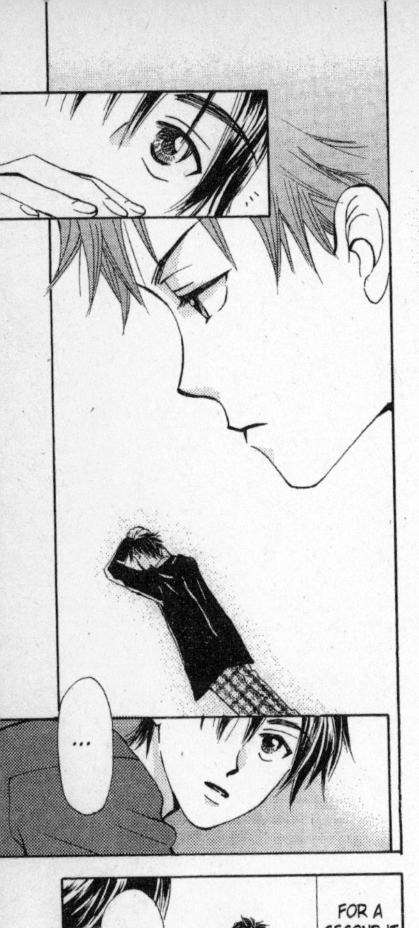
...

FOR A SECOND IT SEEMED...
SAKA-MOTO...

I HEARD YOU TALKING ABOUT TRANSFERRING BEFORE...
...ARE YOU FROM A STRICT HOUSE-HOLD?
YEAH...

IT'S LIKE WHAT DAD SAYS IS LAW.
IF HE SAYS JUMP, YOU JUMP.
THE SCHOOLS I GO TO ARE USUALLY CHOSEN BY HIM.
YOU NOTICED THAT?
AND I GUESS YOU DON'T LIKE IT, HUH?
I DON'T CARE IF THE SCHOOL'S ALL BOYS OR COED...
...BUT IT DOESN'T HAVE A TRACK TEAM.
?
I COULDN'T CARE LESS IF IT'S FAMOUS OR WILL SET ME UP FOR LIFE...
ALL I WANT IS TO GO TO A SCHOOL WHERE I CAN RUN!

SO YOU RUN TRACK?
YEAH...
I'VE BEEN TO PREFECTURAL FINALS.
IN THE 100 AND 200 METER HURDLES.
ARE YOU GOING TO GIVE UP?
...
THERE'S SOMEONE I KNOW! WE'RE REALLY CLOSE!
AND THAT PERSON IS FIGHTING A FATHER WHO WANTS NOTHING MORE THAN TO CRUSH HIS OWN CHILD'S DREAM!
I HAVE THINGS I WANT TO DO, TOO!
I CAN'T STAND PEOPLE WHO GIVE UP AND DO NOTHING!
DREAMS AREN'T MEANT TO BE THROWN AWAY!
VI SH

IF YOU'RE SERIOUS ABOUT YOUR DREAM, SAKA-MOTO...
...YOU SHOULD TRY TO FIND A WAY OUT OF YOUR SITUATION.
...
SHF
IF YOU THINK IT'S EMBARRASSING, IT JUST MEANS YOU DON'T HAVE CONFIDENCE IN YOURSELF.
GAM PH
?!
I REALLY DO LIKE YOU!!

EH?!
I DOUBT THERE'S ANOTHER GIRL IN THE WORLD WHO COULD YELL AT A GUY LIKE THAT!
WAIT--
?!
HEY, I MEAN IT! GO OUT WITH ME!
GLOM
WHY IS THIS HAPPENING?
THIS GUY'S A WEIRDO!
YOU'RE HAVING FUN, HUH, SAKA-MOTO?

!
YOU FOUND YOURSELF A GIRL ALREADY?
HEY!
LOOK AT THAT!
YEAH, A NICE ONE TOO!
?
WHAT'S WITH THESE GUYS?
THEY'RE A DIFFERENT GROUP THAN BEFORE.
Bad vibes
HEY, COME BE OUR GIRL.
grin
grin
IT'S PERFECT! AFTER TODAY WE'LL NEVER SEE EACH OTHER AGAIN, RIGHT?
WE'LL HAVE YOU BACK IN TWO...THREE HOURS TOPS!
WHA-- ?
DON'T GIVE ME THIS BS!
NOT A CHANCE, GUYS.
WE JUST PLEDGED OUR ETERNAL LOVE.
THERE HE GOES AGAIN...
YOU WANT ME TO KNOCK YOU ACROSS THE PARK?
REALLY ?
THEN WE *HAVE* TO ACT NOW.
SHF
WHOOSH

WE'LL JUST BORROW HER FOR A BIT.
!!
WHAT'S YOUR PROB-LEM?
LET ME GO!
YOU'RE A LIVE ONE!
SETTLE DOWN!
haw haw
YOU THINK YOU'RE SO SMART!
I THINK IT'S TIME I THREW A GOING AWAY PARTY ON YOUR FACE!
!
DONK

OWW !!
TMP
WHUMP
AH!
LISTEN CHICKIE...
ZWOO

THAKK
!
?!
VSSH
...!!
WHAT'S WITH THIS WOMAN?
NEVER MIND, JUST GRAB HER!
WHAMMM
I GOT NOTHING TO DO WITH THIS!
BAMMM
SKFFL SKFFL
...
DAMMIT!
I SHOULD NEVER HAVE WORN A SKIRT!
...

I CAN SEE YOUR PANTIES!!
JIKK
GRABB
huff huff
!
YOU ARE A GIRL AFTER ALL!
DAMN!
MIURA-CHAN!
YOU FOOL!
HEH HEH HEH! I'D EXPECT SAKAMOTO TO HAVE A GIRL LIKE YOU!
THROB THROB
LOOK AT WHAT YOU DID TO ME!
LET'S GET THIS CLEAR!
I'VE GOT NOTHING TO DO WITH SAKAMOTO!
YOU THINK THAT'LL MAKE UP FOR WHAT YOU'VE DONE?!
chatter chatter
WHO'S WINNING?
THE GIRL, MAYBE?
WHAT I'M GONNA DO TO YOU--
GANCH

WHAT THE HELL ARE YOU DOING?
!
SHIF
SHUMPH
UFF!
MAKOTO!!
DAMN YOU!
LET G--
OWWW!!
TWST

WHOSE GIRL DO YOU THINK YOU'RE PAWING, BOYS?
SHF
SHF
SHF
...!!
LET'S GO!
TMP
TMP
WOW! HE MADE THEM RUN AWAY WITH JUST ONE PHRASE!
...
SLUMP
WHAT THE HELL WERE *YOU* DOING?!
hm?
I-I'M SORRY!
THINGS HAPPENED, AND I...
MIURA-CHAN!

I'M SORRY THINGS GOT SO WEIRD!
IS THIS THE ONE YOU WERE TALKING ABOUT BEFORE?
UH...
YEAH, HE IS...
UM...

...
...REAL-LY?

BZZT
...
BZZT
BZZT
...?

SST

SORRY I PUSHED YOU AROUND.
HERE'S YOUR SCHOOL I.D.
BUT WHEN YOU TALKED ABOUT DREAMS, I DECIDED ONE THING...
?
FROM NOW ON, I'M TAKING ON THE CHALLENGE, AND I WON'T GIVE UP.
I'LL STAND UP TO MY DAD AND GO FOR THE GOAL!

...
I GET THE FEEL-ING...
...HE WASN'T JUST TALKING ABOUT TRACK.
SEE YA!
IT LOOKS LIKE YOU HAD A BALL WHILE I WASN'T LOOKING.
YOU'RE WRONG!
I HATED EVERY MINUTE OF IT!
YOU WERE TALKING ABOUT DREAMS, RIGHT?
A PRETTY FUN CONVER-SATION.
DUMMY!
HEY! THE GUY HAS CONFI-DENCE PROBLEMS!

SO AS AN EXAMPLE, I TALKED ABOUT YOU.
I DRESSED HIM DOWN SAYING HOW A PERSON WHO IS REALLY CLOSE TO ME WOULD NEVER BACK AWAY FROM A CHALLENGE.
SORRY I TALKED ABOUT YOU BEHIND YOUR BACK.
...

NOW HE'S MAD!
I'M SORRY FOR RUINING OUR DATE!
TURN AROUND AND LOOK AT ME!
MA-KO!
MA-KO!
MA--

...
HE DID IT TO ME AGAIN!
HA HA HA
ITO-SAN, YOU ARE SO MUCH FUN!

WE'VE STILL GOT A LITTLE TIME BEFORE CURFEW.
THE REST OF THE DAY CAN BE FOR US, RIGHT?

...
BUT I'M NEVER WEARING THIS UNIFORM AGAIN UNTIL I GRADUATE!

ARE YOU COM-PLAINING ABOUT THAT *AGAIN?*
IT DOESN'T LOOK GOOD ON ME, AND I GET DRAGGED INTO THESE WEIRD SITUATIONS!
IT'S EVEN BAD FOR FIGHTING!
ABOUT THAT, ACTU-ALLY...

ITO-SAN, YOU'RE A WOMAN OF MANY CHARMS.
EVEN JUST NOW, YOU WERE DOING YOUR BEST TO HELP OUT A STRANGER.
PUT ALL OF YOUR NICE POINTS TO-GETHER...
...AND YOU'RE SOMEONE EVERYONE IS DRAWN TO!
BESIDES, YOU LOOK CUTE IN YOUR UNIFORM.
ARE YOU SAYING YOU WANT ME TO WEAR IT AGAIN?
...
IF I DO, PROTECTING ME IS YOUR RESPON-SIBILITY!
YES, YOUR HIGH-NESS.

THE NARITA HOUSEHOLD.
AH!
Sending presents from Hokkaido. Makoto.
HEH!
THIRD DAUGHTER • AKANE (22) MAKEUP ARTIST
FATHER, WE HAVE A POSTCARD FROM MAKOTO.
SHF
I'LL LOOK AT IT LATER. LEAVE IT OVER THERE.
HE SAYS HE'S IN HOK-KAIDO.
FATHER • MASUMI (49) MARTIAL ARTIST MASTER OF A CHINESE MARTIAL ARTS DOJO
I'M OFF, FATHER.
TSU-BAKI...

-Behind the Scenes Story- ③

This trip was the first time I ever went to the Hidaka Kentucky Farm! I love horses, or I should say that I love animals! And it was the first time I ever rode a horse! The horse just walked, but it sure did sway a lot! I could do nothing but admire those horses that took so many people for rides! Good boys!

OOH..

I wanted to draw this kind of scene in the manga, but it wouldn't fit in the story. It was here that some students on their school excursions came to sightsee, and I took lots of pictures of it! (The outside of the bus.)

Those are some of the weird things you do as a manga-ka.

I dragged my sister along. →

OH, GOD!
I TOOK A WHOLE ROLL OF FILM.

GOING TO A RESTAURANT WITH THAT FIANCE OF YOURS?
TRY NOT TO BE RUDE.
YES, FATHER.
GLINT
SECOND DAUGHTER • TSUBAKI (24) HIGH SCHOOL TEACHER
TSUBAKI, WE GOT A POSTCARD TODAY...
TAK TAK
SORRY, I HAVE NO TIME.
HOLD IT UNTIL AFTER, OKAY?
...FROM MAKO-TO.
ZWOOM
KYAA! LOOK AT MAKO-CHAN'S HAND-WRITING!!
WHEEE!
WOOOW! A PICTURE! WHAT'S THE PICTURE OF?
AH!
A PHOTO-BOOTH PICTURE!
...
to: Akane Narita
from
OPEN
FROM SAKURA?
YOU GOT A LETTER TOO, AKANE?
THAT DOESN'T HAPPEN VERY OFTEN.
YEAH, FROM AN OLD SCHOOL-MATE.
TMP TMP
PROBABLY ABOUT THE ALUMNI ASSOCIA-TION.
REAL-LY?
MOTHER • RISA NARITA HALF BRITISH/HALF JAPANESE.

haven't written you in so long
and we're finally here!
don't know how Hokkaido will
and write to me, okay?
from Sakura Sugiyama
KACHAK
dmp
...
I KNEW IT.
IT'S FROM SAKURA.
KACHIK

HOKKAIDO • HIDAKA KENTUCKY FARM
...
DOOOOM

WHY ARE WE ALWAYS GOING TO THE SAME PLACE AS HIS SCHOOL?!
CHATTER CHATTER
CHATTER
WE'RE PLAGUED WITH SCHOOL EXCUR-SIONS!

IT WOULD HELP IF SOMEBODY DIDN'T DROP HER SCHOOL I.D.
I'LL NEVER DROP IT AGAIN!
YOU DON'T HAVE TO BRING IT UP EVERY TIME!
THEN LET ME SEE YOUR I.D.!
FWIK
AH! IT'S IN ITS PROPER I.D. CASE!
YOU JUST DON'T TAKE CARE OF YOURS.
?
Izumi no Mori Little Theater
The Seven Sightseers

WHAT'S THIS? A THEATER TICKET?
YEAH...
IT'S A GOOD LUCK PIECE.
HM...
SHT
WH--
WHAT IS THIS PICTURE ?!
IS THIS A LITTLE MAKOTO?
HOW OLD WERE YOU IN THIS?
YOU'RE SO DARN CUTE!!
AND THOSE ARE YOUR SISTERS NEXT TO YOU?
YEAH, I WAS...
...11 YEARS OLD.
...
...

SST
MAKO-TO?
!
YOU'RE FROM THE SAKURA-GA-OKA HIGH SCHOOL DRAMA CLUB...
...MAKOTO AMANO-SAN, AREN'T YOU?
?!
MAKO... DO YOU KNOW HER?
...
AND YOU ARE...?
heh!

I'VE MISSED YOU SO MUCH, MAKOTO! ♡
WA!
EH?!
WHOOM

WHAT?!
EYAAA!
KER-WHUMP
I THOUGHT YOU'D BE HERE!
I'M SO GLAD AKANE TOLD ME!
WAIT...
ITO-SAN, ARE YOU ALL RIGHT?
...
WHA--?
EH?!
Caught in the crash
HEARD IT FROM AKANE-SAN?
WHO IS THIS?
AH!
YOU'RE NOT "ITO-SAN," ARE YOU?!
IT'S TRUE! YOU DO HAVE A "GALLANT" FACE!
ZWI
?!

ARRIVAL IN HOKKAIDO

"There was a massive heat wave in Hokkaido in '99," is what the news said, but it really was hot! Still... it wasn't a sticky heat like they have on the Kantô plain (Tokyo), but rather a clear, refreshing heat! It's a heat that's easier to take. I'm jealous of them! The view on Mount Hakodate is just gorgeous! But Emura almost fell, again!

SLIP
GULP

That's me on mountains!

I know that the stairs slope sharply, but...When I was a high school student, I had a spectacular fall from a staircase and wound up with small stones in my hand.

THERE'S SOME-THING IN THERE.
EH?!
Friend

THE INN

It's been too long since I was able to relax so much while still on the job!

WANT TO GO TO THE BATHS?
LET'S WATCH SOME TV, THEN GO.
OK

What did I come all the way to Hokkaido for?! ...then, while we were watching TV, my sister suddenly...

BOINK

AAAAAH!!

To be continued...

THE WAY YOU PUT ON MAKEUP IS GOOD, BUT...
WHY DON'T YOU HANG WITH ME FOR A WHILE?!
TEE HEE HEE HEE
AAH!
RRRING
WHAT'S GOING ON, MAKO?!
RRRING
HEY!!

EYAAAAH!!
Chik
HELLO?

MAKOTO? I'M SORRY IT TOOK ME SO LONG TO GET IN CONTACT.
JUST TO LET YOU KNOW, I GOT A LETTER FROM BIG-SISTER SAKURA TODAY...
THEN I GAVE HER A CALL ON MY CEL PHONE...

SHE SAYS THAT SHE MOVED TO HOKKAIDO.
AND I TOLD HER THE ITINERARY FOR YOUR SCHOOL EXCURSION. I REALIZED THAT SHE JUST MIGHT COME TO SEE YOU...
...

CRAFT SHOP
Merry-Mary

SMILE
ELDEST DAUGHTER OF THE NARITA HOUSE • SAKURA (25)
I'M SORRY I HAVEN'T BEEN IN CONTACT FOR TWO YEARS.
...
DON'T WORRY! AKANE FILLED ME IN ON THE WHOLE SITUATION.
I'M ON YOUR SIDE!
HMMM... ALL OF YOUR SISTERS ARE BEAUTIFUL, AREN'T THEY?
...
HEY...
YOU'VE GOT A WIG ON, RIGHT?
COULD YOU TAKE THAT OFF FOR A BIT?
!
I'M SORRY, BUT I CAN'T DO THAT.
IT'S OKAY! I'LL LOAN YOU MY HAT AND COAT.
COME ON, PLEASE? ♡
IT'S OKAY! NOBODY'S AROUND!
IT'S ONLY FOR A MOMENT!
...

SHF
GOOD ENOUGH FOR YOU?
THIS WAY, YOUR OLD FACE COMES OUT MORE!
THERE'S THE BEAUTIFUL BLONDE HAIR YOU GOT FROM GRAND-MOTHER!
EH?!
YEAH.
IT'S A RECESSIVE GENE. IN MY FAMILY, I WAS THE ONLY ONE WITH BLONDE HAIR.
Grand-mother
Grand-father
Father
Mother
Sakura
Tsubaki
Akane
Makoto
GRAND-MOTHER WAS BRITISH.
WITH EVERYONE ONLY A QUARTER ENGLISH, THE CHANCES WEREN'T TOO GOOD.
IT'S THE FIRST TIME I'VE HEARD THIS STORY.
THE COLOR'S REAL?!
IT'S NOT THAT IMPORTANT.
SURE IT IS!
I GET IT! SO THAT'S WHY EVERY-ONE'S SO PRETTY!
I NEVER MEN-TIONED IT?
I SAID YOU NEVER DID!
TELL ME THESE THINGS QUICKER!
TEE HEE

hee hee hee
SO NOW YOU'RE TRYING TO BE AN ACTOR?
I NEVER KNEW ABOUT YOU PASSING FOR A GIRL UNTIL AKANE TOLD ME!
AFTER ALL, IT'S BEEN SIX YEARS SINCE I LEFT HOME.
EH?!
YOU DIDN'T STRIKE OUT ON YOUR OWN TWO YEARS AGO...?
NO, NO!
IT'S ALMOST EXACTLY SIX YEARS SINCE I LEFT.
AND I DIDN'T DO ANYTHING SO RESPECT-ABLE AS "STRIKE OUT ON MY OWN."
I ELOPED WITH AN ARTIST.
BUT...
FATHER IS AN OLD-STYLE AUTHORITARIAN. HE'D THINK NOTHING OF ARRANGING A MARRIAGE FOR ME FOR BUSINESS REASONS.
I WAS 19, WITH A NICE BOY-FRIEND...
...AND I WAS SO READY TO RUN AWAY FROM HOME.

...
WOW...
...MA-KOTO'S ATTITUDE TOWARDS HIS SISTER...

...IS REALLY COLD!

SKRRT

I'LL WAIT OUTSIDE.

MAKO?
HEY!
...

HE DOES HATE ME AFTER ALL.
EH?
I WAS THE FIRST TO LEAVE HOME.

AND NEVER ONCE DID I THINK ABOUT WHAT EFFECT IT WOULD HAVE ON THOSE LEFT BEHIND.
AFTER-WARDS, FATHER BECAME EVEN WORSE.
GRADUALLY THEY CAME UNDER MORE AND MORE RESTRIC-TIONS.
HE DIDN'T WANT ANYBODY TO REPEAT WHAT I DID.

?!
ESPE-CIALLY MAKOTO, THE ELDEST MALE.
FATHER WAS UN-BELIEVABLY HARSH.
AFTER I LEFT, THE ENTIRE BURDEN OF THE HOUSE FELL ON THAT CHILD'S SHOULDERS.

"DON'T YOU DARE BRING SHAME ON ME!"
FOR THREE WEEKS, MAKOTO WAS TRAPPED IN THE HOUSE DOING ONLY TRAINING.
HE COULDN'T GO TO SCHOOL... THE PHONE LINE WAS CUT...
IT WAS REALLY BAD.
...
WHAT KIND OF RELATION-SHIP IS THAT?
"AL-THOUGH I LOVE MARTIAL ARTS..."
"...I ALWAYS HATED THAT HOUSE."
HE DID SAY A LITTLE ABOUT HIS HOME LIFE BEFORE...
I BROUGHT THOSE TERRIBLE CONDITIONS DOWN ON HIM.
...BUT I NEVER REALIZED HE WAS SO MISER-ABLE.
DO YOU TALK TO ANYBODY IN THE FAMILY?
I TALK TO AKANE PRETTY OFTEN.
WE'RE BREAKING THE EMBARGO.
I SAW MAKOTO TWO YEARS AFTER I LEFT HOME.

AND AFTER THAT, I MET THEM A LOT, BUT MAKOTO ALWAYS STOOD BEHIND AKANE.
AND HE NEVER LOOKED ME IN THE EYES.
HE'S ASHAMED OF THE STUPID CHOICES I MADE.
?
IF HE ACTUALLY NEVER WANTED TO SEE YOU...
...I DOUBT HE WOULD HAVE GONE ALONG WITH AKANE-SAN IN THE FIRST PLACE.
I CAN'T SAY I'M AN EXPERT ON YOUR FAMILY...
...BUT MAYBE IT WASN'T THAT HE COULDN'T MEET YOUR EYES...
...BUT RATHER THAT HE COULDN'T FIND THE RIGHT WORDS.
HE'S NOT ADULT ENOUGH TO FORGIVE AND FORGET...
...BUT HE CAN'T AVOID YOU LIKE A CHILD ANYMORE.
HE'S STILL SOME-WHERE IN BETWEEN.

RRRRING
RRRRING
RRRRING
YOU WATCH MAKOTO PRETTY CLOSELY, DON'T YOU?
RRRRING
I DON'T THINK HE HATES HIS BIG SISTER.
I'LL GO OUT AND FIND HIM.
I'M SURE IT'S HIS INSECURITIES.
HIS CHILD'S SOUL STRIKES BACK, AND HE GIVES HIS SISTER THE COLD SHOULDER.
"MAKOTO-CHAN IS A GOOD BOY!"

"HIS GRADES ARE TOP OF THE CLASS!"
"HE LISTENS CLOSELY AND DOES HIS BEST!"
"I'M JUST SO JEALOUS"
SAKURA-CHAN?
"MAKOTO-CHAN IS A GOOD BOY!"
NO!
IN REALITY...
IN REALITY...
Morizumi No Mori Little The
The Seven Sightseers
MA-KOTO!
CHK

AH!
ITO-SAN...
WHAT ARE YOU DOING SLEEPING OUT HERE?
YOUR SISTER'S WORRIED ABOUT YOU!
...
YOU HEARD THE STORY, DIDN'T YOU?
MOST OF IT, I GUESS.
THERE IS ONE THING I DON'T GET.
...
...
MAKO... DO YOU HATE YOUR SISTER?
NOT REALLY.
I BEAR A GRUDGE, BUT I DON'T HATE HER.

SAKURA ELOPED WHEN I WAS 11 YEARS OLD.
EH?
ON THE OTHER HAND, THAT'S WHEN I DECIDED ON MY DREAM OF BECOMING AN ACTOR.
A YEAR LATER, I GOT FED UP WITH BEING LOCKED UP IN THAT HOUSE, AND I RAN AWAY.
AKANE BROUGHT ME BACK.
!
THAT WAS THE REASON SHE TOOK ME TO THE THEATER.
...YOU STILL HOLD A GRUDGE?
AH! BUT...
...
IT'S HARD TO ERASE THE FEELINGS FROM ONE'S CHILD-HOOD.
I BEAR A GRUDGE, BUT I AM ALSO GRATEFUL.
WHAT CAN I SAY, IT'S...
...COM-PLICATED.
...
AH HA HA HA
YOU WERE TRYING TO IMITATE ME, RIGHT?
NO, I WASN'T!!
YOU DUMMY! DON'T JINX ME!
SAME TO YOU, ITO-SAN!
heh

...
MA-KOTO?
WHAT A SHAME! YOU'RE GOING TO PUT THE WIG BACK ON?
OH, NO!
I PROMISED FATHER.
VSHH
HEY! HEY!
SHOW HER THE SMILE YOU JUST HAD ON!
An automatic response...
WHY DO YOU WANT TO BE AN ACTOR SO MUCH?
YOU DIDN'T HAVE THAT AMBITION BEFORE I LEFT.
IT WAS TWO YEARS AGO THAT I TOLD FATHER I WANTED TO BE AN ACTOR.
BUT IT'S BEEN MY DREAM SINCE I WAS 12.

"MAKOTO-CHAN IS A GOOD BOY!"
BUT I WAS THE ONE WHO WAS "IMITATING."
...
I ALWAYS THOUGHT THAT "ACTING" WAS IMITATING.
AT LEAST BEFORE I SAW REAL ACTORS.
LIFE BY THE RULES.
I THOUGHT THAT MY LIFE WAS ALREADY DECIDED FOR ME.
I HAD NO GOAL. I JUST PLAYED THE PART OF A GOOD BOY WHO DID WHATEVER MY FATHER PUSHED ME INTO.
BUT THE DAY I ENTERED THE THEATER, EVERYTHING WAS TURNED UPSIDE-DOWN.
THESE ACTORS WERE LIVING A FAR MORE BRILLIANT LIFE...
...THAN I WAS-- A GUY WHOSE WHOLE LIFE WAS AN ACT.
AT THE CHEERS AND APPLAUSE, MY BODY WARMED.
THE EMOTION...THE FEVER THAT HIT ME WHEN I TOOK IN THAT PLAY...
...MADE ME WANT TO GIVE THAT FEELING BACK TO OTHER PEOPLE IN THE FUTURE!
I THOUGHT THAT THE ABILITY OF AN ACTOR TO PLAY A VARIETY OF PARTS WAS THE MOST AMAZING SKILL I HAD EVER SEEN!
LIFE ISN'T SOMETHING THAT'S ALREADY DECIDED FOR YOU!

THAT'S THE VERY BASIS OF ACTING, ISN'T IT?
AND I THOUGHT THERE WAS SOME TALENT THERE. IN ME.
I FOUND A REASON TO LIVE.
AH! HE SAID IT!
THE FIRST STEP TO SELF-RELIANCE.
SO I DECIDED I'D BE AN ACTOR NO MATTER WHAT.
...
YOUR FACE RELAXED A BIT.
YOU DON'T HAVE TO FIX IT!
PEOPLE ACT DIFFERENTLY WHEN NEAR SOMEONE THEY CARE FOR.
!
TEE HEE
WHEN YOU'RE WITH ITO-SAN, YOU TALK MORE AND LAUGH MORE, MAKOTO!
YOU'RE TALLER AND MORE MATURE...
...YOU'VE CHANGED A LOT!
SAKURA!
OH!
WHAT'S UP? YOU SAID TO MEET IN THE COFFEE SHOP!
SORRY! THANK YOU FOR COMING TO PICK ME UP! ♡
EH?
!

THIS BABY IS...
...THE REASON I HAVEN'T KEPT IN TOUCH FOR TWO YEARS.
EH?!
I CAN'T BELIEVE YOU HAVE A CHILD!
NOW WE'RE SETTLED DOWN WITH MY HUSBAND'S FAMILY IN SAPPORO.
I WROTE AKANE ABOUT THAT...
...BUT I HAVEN'T SAID A WORD ABOUT MY BOY YET.
HE'S A LITTLE OVER A YEAR OLD...
WE WERE MARRIED WHEN I WAS TWENTY.
A BOY.
TWENTY? HUH?
...
WE WERE TRAVELING THE WORLD DOING MY ART-WORK...
...BUT IN THE END, HOKKAIDO JUST HAD TO BE OUR HOME.

I MUST SAY, YOU'VE REALLY FILLED OUT, MAKOTO-KUN!
THOROUGH-LY!
THE LINE IS, "YOU'VE REALLY GROWN UP!"
MY GOOFY HUSBAND!
THWA
...
KK
...
SATOSHI, THAT ISN'T YOUR MAMA!
AH HA HA HA HA
CAN I HOLD HIM?
SURE.
GRMP
ITO'S A REAL WOMAN, HUH?
...
"YOU RAN OFF AND ABANDONED US"...
!
...THAT WAS THE GRUDGE I HELD AGAINST YOU.
IN THE END, I DECIDED TO TAKE EXACTLY THE SAME PATH YOU DID.
I CHOSE TO DEFY FATHER AND SEEK MY FREEDOM.

SAKURA, NOW I UNDERSTAND EXACTLY HOW YOU FELT.
AH!
OH, NO! MAKO, THE CLASS GATHERS IN FIVE MINUTES!
WHAT? IT'S THAT LATE ALREADY ?
!
?
GRABB
ITO-SAN, WAIT A SEC-OND!
I WANT YOU TO HAVE THIS!
IT WAS SOMETHING I'VE HAD EVER SINCE I ELOPED.

A PICTURE?
I CAN'T TAKE SOMETHING THIS IMPORTANT...
IT'S FINE! I *WANT* YOU TO HAVE IT!
IN EX-CHANGE, SEND ME VACATION PICTURES!
ESPECIALLY ANY TWO-SHOTS YOU GET!
I'LL BE SURE TO SEND SOME!
...
WHAT HAP-PENED?
I THOUGHT YOU AND MAKOTO WERE ON THE OUTS.
heh heh
WE WERE AT FIRST.
BUT THAT GIRL WAS HERE...
...AND WE WERE ABLE TO TALK FOR THE FIRST TIME IN SIX YEARS.
GWOOOOO

Chatter Chatter
I THINK IT WOULD HAVE BEEN NICE IF YOU SMILED A LITTLE MORE FOR HER.
Chatter Chatter
THIS WAS THE BEST I'VE EVER MANAGED.
HUHHH? I THOUGHT YOU *DIDN'T* HATE HER!
SHE GETS TO ME.
HEY, MIURA!!
GET BACK TO YOUR OWN SEAT!
WE'RE ABOUT TO LAND!
YES, SIR!
SST
!
IT'S MAKO'S STUDENT I.D.
I HAD IT ALL THIS TIME.
fft
"IT'S A GOOD LUCK PIECE."
heh
Student Identification Card
Makoto Amano
I'LL BET THIS TICKET IS...
...A MEMENTO OF WHEN HE RAN AWAY.
IN OTHER WORDS, WHEN HE TOOK BACK HIS LIFE.
I GOT TO HEAR A LOT OF COOL THINGS TODAY!
AND I GOT A NICE PICTURE!
sst

...
HE'S GOT HIS PEEVISH SIDE TOO, HUH?
ha ha ha
I WISH...
...THAT WE COULD SPEND THE DAYS UNTIL GRADUATION IN PEACE.
BUT I DON'T THINK THAT'S GOING TO HAPPEN.
WHAT'RE YOU WRITING, SAKAMOTO?
A CHALLENGE TO MY DAD.
YOU MEAN YOU'RE *NOT* GOING TO TRANSFER OUT?
sKritch
sKritch
DON'T BE STUPID!

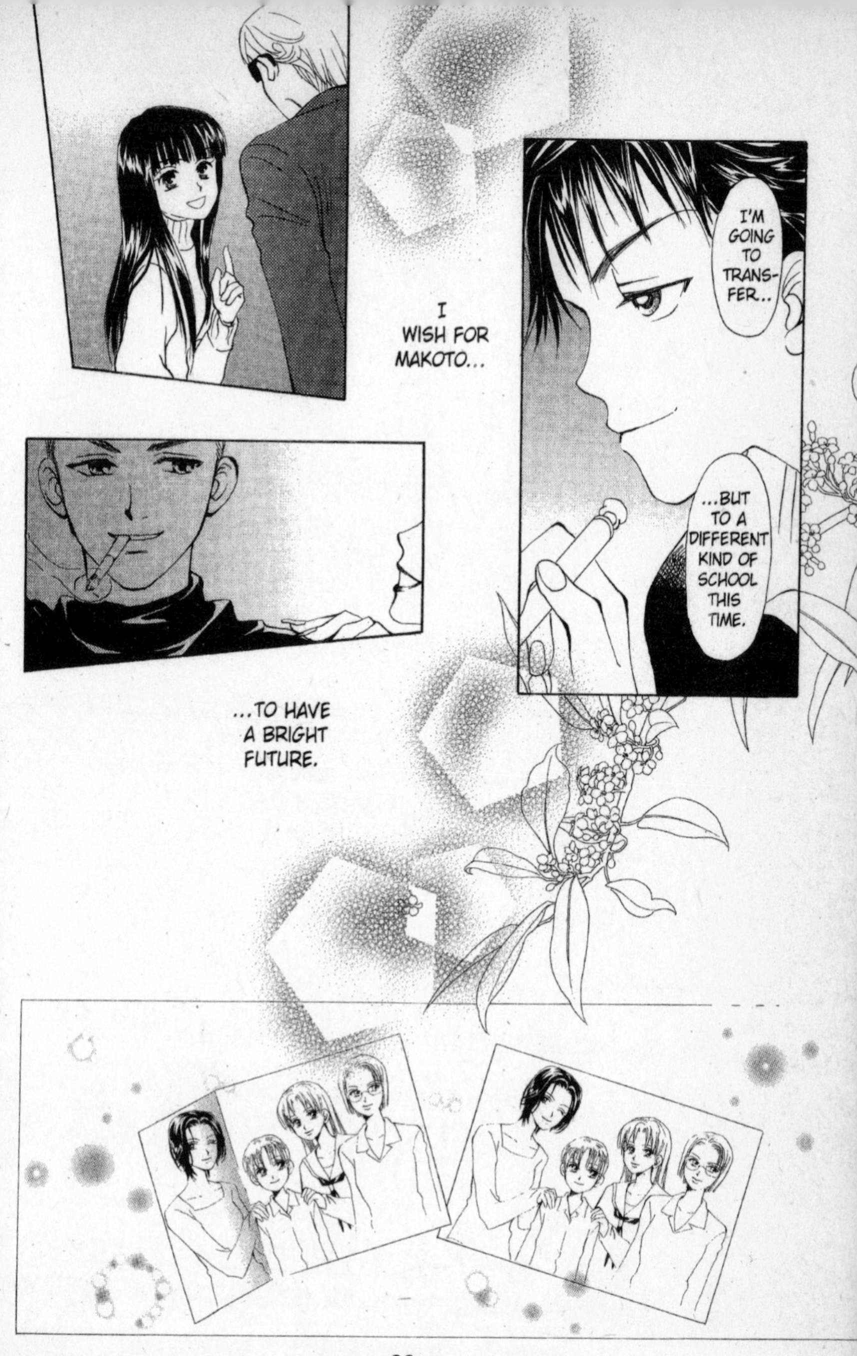
I'M GOING TO TRANS-FER...
...BUT TO A DIFFERENT KIND OF SCHOOL THIS TIME.
I WISH FOR MAKOTO...
...TO HAVE A BRIGHT FUTURE.

W Juliet

"A WHITE CHRISTMAS."
"ON CHRISTMAS EVE..."
"...YOU MAKE A LITTLE STATUE OF A BLUE-EYED ANGEL THAT'S LOOKING TOWARD THE EAST, JUST LIKE THIS."
"BUT BE PRE-PARED..."
"THEN YOU MAKE ONE WISH."
"...BE-CAUSE IF YOU DON'T HAVE..."
"...GOD WON'T GRANT YOUR WISH!"

-Behind the Scenes Story- ④

I made up the story of the snowman-angel. At first, I couldn't make up my mind. I thought maybe I'd come up with a legend of a red-eyed snow rabbit, but the concept seemed to lack something. So I made it into an angel. There just didn't seem to be enough pages to tell the story, so I asked my editor, "Can I please do it in two installments?" He sidestepped the request by saying, "This isn't the kind of subject you can lengthen into two installments!" I guess that's true. So I gave Ito's story precedence and cut back on the Christmas party and contest portions of the plot. If only I had a few more pages... No, if I had them, then I would have had to spend time drawing the extra pages... Argh! But still, the story and color illustration were very popular. I really liked the color illustration for this installment! ♡

THE EYES WOULD BE RUBIES... NAW! THAT WOULD BE TOO EXPENSIVE.

"BUT BE PREPARED FOR IT TO COME TRUE..."
...
HUH? YOU'RE ALREADY AWAKE, ITO?
THEN SHUT OFF YOUR ALARM, WILL YA?
BREAK-FAST IS SERVED ALREADY.
...
BRRRRRRRRR
RRRRRRRRRR
RRRR
"ITO."
MY DREAM WAS OF AN OLD MEMORY...
hmmmm
BUT WHY NOW...
KA-KLIK
IT HAPPENED OVER 10 YEARS AGO.
WHY SHOULD I REMEMBER IT NOW?
KACHAK
AH!

Continued...
BIG SISTER, WHAT'LL WE DO?
YOU'RE TOO LOUD.
WHAT'S WRONG?
All of the sudden...
WHOOSH
Oshare Kôbô presents: Kaoru Wada creating Flower Bottles!!
OUR SCHOOL TEACHER IS ON TV!
A TAPE! WE HAVE TO TAPE THIS!
GET MOM ON THE PHONE!
AAAAAH!
Is it really going to be on?
Wada-sensei is a teacher in our old specialty school. (A school for florists.) Not just a popular florists'-school teacher, but popular throughout the whole world of flowers! Pretty darned famous! There are also a ton of books to Wada-sensei's credit; even without teaching, I doubt the Wada's would go hungry.
Sensei even introduced my sister to Kaori.
Sayaka
Kaori
(Florist School)
The reception on Hokkaido broadcast TV was terrible! So it was a good thing that we got Mom to tape it for us!
Oh, almost all of my old teachers know what I'm doing now!
MAYBE BECAUSE IT SNOWED TODAY, JUST LIKE THEN.
SNOWBALL FIGHT
YAAAAAAY
IT ISN'T OFTEN THAT IT SNOWS ON CHRISTMAS EVE.
IT'S USUALLY IN JANUARY OR FEBRUARY.
THAT'S TRUE.
BUT THIS IS A LUCKY BREAK! WE DON'T HAVE TO TRIM THE TREES!
YOU'RE RIGHT. REAL SNOW IS SO MUCH BETTER THAN TINSEL.
AND IT'S EASIER TO GIVE WHEN IT'S COLD.
smile

Have you seen Wada-sensei? I used a Wada-sensei flower bottle in volume 3!

?
SEE YOU AFTER CLASSES, ITO-SAN!
WHAT DID HE JUST SAY?
TODAY IS CHRISTMAS EVE.
THESE ARE THE LAST CLASSES OF THE SECOND TERM, AND THEN IT'S WINTER VACATION!
PARENT INVITATION
2nd Year, 5th class, Student# 31, Ito Miura
THERE'S A SCHOOL EVENT THIS EVENING...
BOTH STUDENTS AND NON-STUDENTS CAN COME.
AWW! I HATE THIS!
ME TOO.
DON'T MAKE ME LAUGH!

IT'S A CHRISTMAS PARTY.
AAAAAAH!!
BA MM

YES, MIURA? YOU YELLED?
IS SOMETHING WRONG?
...

IT'S NOTHING, SIR.
I SEE. YOU HAD TO GET IN YOUR FINAL COMPLAINT OF THE YEAR?
ha ha
ha ha
ha
KATUNK
DUMMY!
ZHAPAPAN
DAMMIT! A CHRISTMAS PRESENT FOR MAKOTO!!
I DON'T HAVE ANYTHING FOR HIM!
WHAT'LL I DO! IT HAS TO BE ON CHRISTMAS EVE OR CHRISTMAS DAY, RIGHT?
AND IF I GIVE IT ON THE 25TH, IT'LL BE LIKE I FORGOT!
THIS IS BAD!
"ON CHRIST-MAS EVE ..."
"...YOU MAKE A LITTLE STATUE OF A BLUE-EYED ANGEL."
"THEN YOU MAKE ONE WISH."

DINNNG
HUH?
DONNNG
WHERE'S ITO-SAN?
DINNNG
DONNNG
I DON'T KNOW.
THE MINUTE HOMEROOM WAS OVER, SHE SHOT OUT OF HERE.
?!
SHE PROBABLY STOPPED OFF AT HOME.
IN A COUPLE OF HOURS THE CHRISTMAS PARTY STARTS.
MAYBE SHE'S GOT THINGS TO PREPARE.
I'LL BE BACK ON TIME!
SHE LEFT WITHOUT SAYING GOOD-BYE...
TMP TMP
MAKOTO-SAN! MAKOTO-SAN!
YOUR SISTER IS HERE!
!
MAKOTO! THANKS FOR INVITING ME!
IT'S REALLY OKAY FOR ME TO DO MAKEUP FOR THE DRAMA CLUB GIRLS?
WOW! SHE'S SO PRETTY! THEY COULD BE TWINS!
EVERYBODY NEEDS MAKEUP HELP TONIGHT!
chatter chatter
SOME KIND OF PLAY?
NO...

THE WHOLE DRAMA CLUB IS GOING TO THE PARTY IN COSTUME!
"BLUE-EYED ANGEL."
THAT'S LAPIS, HUH?
CHALING
heh heh
MAYBE GIVING A "FEELING" AS A PRESENT WOULD BE BETTER THAN A "THING"...
I'D LIKE IT TO BE SOMETHING SPECIAL.
THAT'S RIGHT! SNOW HARDLY EVER FALLS ON CHRISTMAS EVE!
I MIGHT BE ABLE TO MAKE THAT CHARM!
chatter
chatter
chatter
chatter
BUT IT SEEMS THERE WAS ONE OTHER THING...
HUH?
"...IF YOU DON'T HAVE..."
"...GOD WON'T GRANT YOUR WISH!"
"BUT..."
"BE PREPARED..."
"...ITO."

HAVE WHAT?
TA-DAAAAH! ♥♥
NOW THAT'S CUTE. ♡
RED RIDING HOOD AND SNOW WHITE.
IT SUITS YOU PERFECT-LY!
THANK YOU SO MUCH FOR DOING MY HAIR!
NOT AT ALL!
I'M NEXT!
I'M SO JEALOUS! ♥ ♥
HUMPH! WHO NEEDS A MAKEUP ARTIST?
SHF
IS THAT WHAT YOU WANT, YOUR HIGHNESS?

DID SHE PAY FOR THAT HERSELF?
THAT COSTUME?
HO HO HO! SHALL WE PROCEED?
I DON'T WANNA BE SEEN WITH HER.
DO
OOM
OF COURSE IT IS! NOBODY IS BETTER AT MAKEUP THAN ME!
CERTAINLY NOT SOME SECOND-RATE HACK LIKE MAKOTO AMANO'S RELATIVE!
Elizabeth the First
KACHIK
MS. ITO, THE TOAST IS IN 15 MINUTES!
AH!
MIURA-SEMPAI?
WHOOOAH!
YOU LOOK GREAT, ITO-SAN!
ITO-SAN, WHO ARE YOU DRESSED UP AS?
NAPO-LEON.
CHATTER CHATTER
IT'S TERR-IFIC!
CHATTER CHATTER
TSK! WHAT'S A GIRL WEARING THAT FOR?
Ko-chan
BUT I WAS SURPRISED AT ALL THE COSTUMES WE MANAGED TO GET!
ALL OF THEM PRETTY CLASSY!
MOST OF THEM ARE BORROWED.
TOKI-CHAN'S COLLEGE LET US USE THEIRS.

...DOES THAT MEAN THAT TOKI-CHAN WILL BE HERE?
EH ?!
GAK
IMPOSSIBLE, I'D SAY. HE SAID HE HAD DATES WITH THREE GIRLS.
SO HE'S DONE IT AGAIN?
NOW EVERYBODY WHO'S READY, LET'S GO!!
ITO-SAN, SHALL I DO YOUR MAKEUP?
I MIGHT BE ABLE IMPROVE IT... MAYBE.
heh
I'M FINE. I'M DRESSED AS A GUY ANYWAY.
AND I DON'T *WANT* TO LOOK ANY MORE MANLY.
...
I HEARD YOU MET MY SISTER SAKURA IN HOKKAIDO.
YES.
HOW DID SHE LOOK?
...
SHE LOOKED LIKE THE HAPPIEST GIRL IN THE WORLD.
I'M GLAD.
I ASKED MAKO, BUT HE WOULDN'T SAY A WORD.
THAT GUY...
...
SHE LOOKED HAPPY.
REALLY HAPPY.
SOME-DAY...

...IT'D BE NICE IF I COULD BE THAT HAPPY.
ITO-KUN, I FORGOT TO ASK... WHERE'S MAKO-CHAN?
PRO-BABLY GETTING CHANGED.
BUT SHE SHOULD BE FINISHED SOON...
kachak
smile
I WANTED TO WAIT UNTIL MOST OF THE PEOPLE WERE GONE.
...AT LEAST THAT WAS THE PLAN, BUT THERE ARE STILL PLENTY HERE, HUH?
MAKOTO-SAN?!?!
YOU'RE BEAUTIFUL!!!
SHE REALLY IS JULIET!!
WHOOOOAAHH!
WHO MADE YOU UP?
I DID IT MYSELF.
YOU LEARNED LIKE A LITTLE SISTER SHOULD!
TOO BAD HE'S A BROTHER.
OH, BUT WHAT'LL I DO?

ITO-SAN, WHERE DID YOU GO BEFORE?
JUST TO PICK UP SOMETHING I FORGOT.
ha ha!
...
I'VE GOT THE LAPIS STONES...
NO MATTER HOW HARD I TRY!
BUT I STILL DON'T REMEMBER WHAT ELSE I SHOULD HAVE!
AHHHHHH!!
?

I GOTTA REMEMBER BEFORE THE PARTY ENDS!!
SOON IT'LL BE THE YEAR 2000!!
YAAA-A
AAAAY
Merry X-mas!!!
WOW! LOOK AT THAT CHRISTMAS TREE!
IT'S HUGE!!
IT'LL LOOK EVEN BETTER WHEN IT GETS DARKER!
AND THE LIGHTS COME ON.
IT'S EVEN TRIMMED WITH PROPER SNOW!

ha!
WHAT IS THIS? A SNOW HUT WITH AN ODEN SIGN?
ODEN
I LIKE ODEN AT CHRISTMAS!!
HEY, THEY'RE PLAYING POKER OVER THERE.
YEAH, IF YOU BEAT FIVE OTHER PEOPLE, YOU GET CAKE.
REALLY? LET'S GO!
WHEN'S THE BEAUTY CONTEST?
CHATTER
CHATTER
CHATTER
CHATTER
WELL LOOK AT THIS. THEY ACTUALLY HAVE SOME ACTIVITIES.
THE CHRISTMAS COMMITTEE TAKES CARE OF IT.
IT'S GOT BOOTHS LIKE A SMALL CULTURAL FESTIVAL.
Chatter
REALLY?
Chatter
MIURA-SEMPAI! POSE FOR US!
OKAY!
KACHIK
NOBODY WANTED A GROUP PICTURE!
WAY TO GO DRAMA CLUB!
A Famous Christmas Tradition
YOSHIRO, WHO ARE YOU?
DADDY LONG-LEGS.
WELL, YOUR LEGS ARE TOO LONG!
DING DONG DING DONG

There are more than 20 clubs.
TAK TAK
I'M HERE TO INFORM EVERYONE OF THE BEAUTY CONTEST THAT STARTS AT 6:00 PM.
ANYONE CAN ENTER, BUT BECAUSE OF THE LARGE NUMBER OF POTENTIAL APPLICANTS, WE WOULD LIKE ONLY ONE APPLICANT PER CLUB.
CHATTER CHATTER
OH!
WHO DO YOU THINK WILL BE THE CHRISTMAS EVE QUEEN?
Mike
WHOEVER THE QUEEN IS WILL HAVE A GREAT PRIZE TO LOOK FORWARD TO...
A PAIR OF MATCHING BRACELETS, THE PERFECT CHRISTMAS PRESENT!
WHOAH!
18 CARET GOLD?
WOOOW!
ALL APPLICANTS SHOULD GATHER ON THE THIRD FLOOR OF "BUILDING A" 15 MINUTES BEFORE THE CONTEST!
AH!
TMP
ITO-SAN!

SORRY, MAKO! I GOT SOMETHING TO DO!
NOW I REMEMBER!!
I WANT TO DO IT!
YO-SHIRO! WHO IS OUR ENTRANT FOR THE CONTEST?
?
UM... PROBABLY MAKOTO-SAN.
?!
HUH?!
I NEED THAT PRIZE!!
BUT SHE HAS TO WIN FIRST.
AKANE-SAN, CAN YOU DO MY MAKEUP?
QUICKLY?
SURE. LEAVE IT TO ME!
THIS'LL BE FUN!
IT SHOULD BE OKAY, RIGHT? ITO-SAN IS RATHER PRETTY.
I APPROVE OF IT!
SO DO I!
WHAT'S PRETTY ABOUT HER?
WHO WOULD WANT TO SEE A GUY COMPETE?
KYAA
SHE'S NO BETTER THAN AVERAGE!
KYAA
SHE'S PRETTY! AND WITH A PRO DOING THE MAKE-UP, EVEN A GUY COULD WIN!

THERE ISN'T A PERSON IN THE WORLD WHO *WOULDN'T* TURN AND STARE.
CHATTER
!
AH!

MIURA?!
?
YEAH ?
WHAT DO YOU THINK? WE WANTED TO DO A JULIET OF THE FAR EAST!
I THOUGHT SHE'D BE PERFECT NEXT TO MAKOTO!
...
SHE THOUGHT RIGHT!
WOOOOW!!
MAKO, AFTER THE BEAUTY CONTEST IS OVER, I WANT TO TALK TO YOU!
SHE'S SO CUTE!
MEET ME IN THE PARK OUT BACK, OKAY?
?
OKAY.
ITO-KUN, I'M IN LOVE ALL OVER AGAIN!! ♡♡
MS. ITO?
WA!
HUGG
WELL, GENTLE-MEN?
WHAT'S YOUR OPINION?
UM...
UH...
SHE MAY WIN.
YEAH.
OKAY, I'M OFF TO REGISTER.
Ito
Drama Club Women
BE CARE-FUL!
Every one
RIGHT! NOW THAT'S DONE...
...I'M SURE TO GET MY HANDS ON THOSE BRACELETS!
GO!
ZOOM
SHE'S STILL THE SAME ON THE INSIDE.
TRUE THAT.

HYUUUU
UUU
Building B
Building A
Present position
Registration
Back Door
Main Entrance
Center Courtyard
THIS IS A PAIN! THE STAIRS ARE SO FAR AWAY!
I GUESS THE ONLY OPEN DOORS ARE THE MAIN ENTRANCE AND THE BACK DOOR.
NO MATTER WHAT, I'M GOING TO HAVE TO GO THROUGH THE SNOW!
AREN'T THERE ANY SHORT-CUTS?
I'M LOCKED OUT.
MY ONLY DIRECT ROUTE.
THE BRIDGE CLOSES AT 5:00 PM IN WINTER.
!
HEY!
HYUUUUUUUU
LOOK AT IT COME DOWN!
IT'S ALMOST LIKE A BLIZZARD!
CAN THEY EVEN HOLD THE CONTEST OUTSIDE?
I DON'T KNOW...
GISH
GISH
THEY HAVEN'T MADE ANY ANNOUNCE-MENTS...
I HOPE IT'LL BE OKAY.
SNAPP

BASHINK
AAAAAAAH!!
?!
A BLACK-OUT?
ZLIPP
!

FWIK

THEY FIXED IT!
Phewwww
BUT WHAT CAUSED IT?
A DOWNED POWER LINE, MAYBE?
Chatter Chatter
KAK KAK
WE HAVE AN UPDATE...
...DUE TO THE WEATHER CONDITIONS, THE BEAUTY CONTEST SCHEDULED FOR 6:00 PM HAS BEEN CANCELED...
ONLY MAKES SENSE.
OKAY, THEN WE'LL...
...IS WHAT I SHOULD BE ANNOUN-CING...
...BUT IT'S ONLY BEEN MOVED TO THE GYM-NASIUM.
...
THEY'RE STILL HOLDING IT?
TO REPEAT THE UP-DATE...
...
DUE TO WEATHER...
ITO-SAN NEVER REGIS-TERED?!
EH?

NO. NOTHING HERE.
BUT IT'S BEEN FOREVER SINCE SHE LEFT THE CLUB ROOMS.
THERE'S ONLY FIVE MINUTES UNTIL CUT-OFF.
MAYBE SHE DECIDED AGAINST IT RIGHT AFTER SHE LEFT.
NOT A CHANCE!
YOU SAW HOW MUCH SHE WANTED THOSE BRACELETS!
?!
ANYWAY, WE'LL GO LOOKING FOR HER.
TMP
TMP
...
...
HOW MANY CONTES-TANTS DO YOU HAVE?
LET'S SEE... 18 AT PRESENT.
THE TOP BEAUTY WINS THE PRIZE, RIGHT?
EH?!

"THEY SAY YOU GET ONE WISH..."
"...IF YOU MAKE A LITTLE STATUE OF A BLUE-EYED ANGEL ON CHRISTMAS EVE."
OH...
...IT'S THAT DREAM AGAIN.
I FORGOT THAT MY HAIR WAS SO LONG AT THAT AGE.
"TRY IT WHEN YOU GET OLDER."
"BUT ONCE YOU MAKE YOUR WISH, YOU CAN'T TOUCH IT UNTIL MORNING."
"WHAT ABOUT YOU, MOMMY?"
"DID YOU MAKE A WISH?"
"I SURE DID! AND JUST AFTERWARDS, YOUR FATHER PROPOSED!"
"SO I BELIEVE!"
A LIGHT?
"AND DON'T EVER GIVE UP ON YOUR WISH!"
"NOW..."
"YOU HAVE TO GO..."

"ITO!"
AH!
ITO-SAN!!
I REMEMBER...
...I SLIPPED FROM THE EMERGENCY EXIT STAIRS...
?
I'M SURPRISED YOU'RE STILL SO WARM!
HEY! HAVE YOU BEEN BURIED THERE ALL THIS TIME?
ARE YOU ALL RIGHT? WE HAVE TO GET YOU TO THE CLUB ROOM!
ANYBODY ELSE WOULD DIE!
GO GET WARM THINGS READY FOR HER!
...
HUH?
RIGHT!
WHAT ABOUT THE CONTEST ?!
OH...

THAT ENDED WHILE WE WERE LOOKING FOR YOU.
HUP
IT'S BEEN OVER FOR A GOOD HALF AN HOUR.
"MAKO...
"...AFTER THE BEAUTY CONTEST IS OVER, I WANT TO TALK TO YOU!"
OH, NO!
MIURA...?
I PROMISED!!

...
WHAT DID I EXPECT?
IT'S BEEN MORE THAN 30 MINUTES SINCE IT ENDED.
AND I NEVER GOT THE BRACELETS, EITHER.
BUT...
SHF
SHF
SHF
SHF
MAYBE EVEN AN UNFINISHED ANGEL...
KLIK
KLIK
ONLY NOW DO I GET COLD!
BRRR
I WONDER IF IT'LL COME TRUE...
WHAT'RE YOU DOING?

MAKO!
YOU WERE RIGHT THERE?
I BOUGHT YOU SOME HOT COFFEE.
WHERE HAVE YOU BEEN ALL THIS TIME?
EVERY-BODY WAS SO WORRIED ABOUT YOU.
I GOT A LITTLE BURIED IN THE SNOW.
?!
IT DOESN'T MATTER. I'LL TELL YOU LATER.
SST
HERE. I WENT AND GOT THESE FOR YOU.
EH?
YOU WERE SO ANXIOUS TO GET THEM, RIGHT?
THESE GOLD BRACELETS?
AH!!
YOU ENTERED THE BEAUTY CONTEST?!
A pair
JUST FILLING IN FOR YOU.
IT WAS A LANDSLIDE. I GOT 460 VOTES OUT OF 500.
CONGRATULATIONS! MISS SAKARA-GA-OKA
WOW!

I REALLY WANTED...
...TO GET THE BRACELETS MYSELF.
?
THANKS, MAKO!!
THIS WILL COMPLETE THE ANGEL!
SHF SHF
THE LEGEND SAYS THAT IF YOU MAKE A BLUE-EYED ANGEL OF SNOW ON CHRISTMAS EVE, YOUR WISH WILL BE GRANTED!
SO, I'LL MAKE ONE.
BUT WITHOUT ONE OF THESE...
GOD WON'T RECOGNIZE IT AS AN ANGEL.
Angel?
AN ANGEL'S HALO?
ha ha
I WONDER WHO WAS THE FIRST TO THINK UP THIS ONE!
AACHOO!
FWOOF

MY CHRISTMAS PRESENT TO YOU.
A SHAWL?
!
IT *IS* PRETTY COLD OUT.
"IT'S EASIER TO GIVE WHEN IT'S COLD."
TH-- THANK YOU!
THIS IS WHAT HE WAS TALKING ABOUT!
ANWW
MY WISH IS...
...FIRST TO GRADUATE SAFELY FROM HIGH SCHOOL...
...THEN TO ENTER A THEATER TROOP AS AN ACTOR...
...AND TO LIVE SIDE-BY-SIDE WITH THE WOMAN I LOVE.

AND YOU, ITO-SAN?
...
THE EXACT SAME THING! PRETTY PATHETIC, RIGHT?
THINK IT'LL COME TRUE?
SURE IT WILL!
WE'VE GOT DOUBLE WISH POWER ON THE SAME WISH!
YOU'RE PROB-ABLY RIGHT.
PLEASE, SOMEDAY...

...IT'D BE NICE TO BE LIKE MY MOTHER FROM MY DREAMS...
...OR LIKE SAKURA-SAN...
...I WOULD LIKE HAPPINESS TO COME TO ME.
THAT IS MY PRAYER FOR NOW, AND FOR THE FUTURE.
The Next Day
WHY ARE *WE* THE ONES TO CATCH COLD?!
KOFF KOFF
SHE WAS BURIED IN THE SNOW FOR TWO HOURS!
GAHMFF
CAN'T SHE JUST CATCH A LITTLE COLD?!
HARUMPH HARUMPH
...
IS SHE SUPER GIRL?
WHAT'S THAT?!
YEAH, YEAH. LET'S GO OFF AND BE HAPPY.

-Behind the Scenes Story- ⑤

This time, not only did I have absolutely no time, but I was feeling sick as a dog! (My bronchitis acted up again!) I couldn't stop coughing and oh the backaches... It was a fever! But with the deadline so close, I was scared to take my temperature. (I figure it was about 38 C (100.5 F).) When I had finished, I went to the hospital for a quick shot. I was shocked at the size of the thing! Were they that big before? When I was a student, I was the picture of health, but since I became a manga artist, I've become a weakling! In two years, my bronchitis has acted up three times. This kind of thing doesn't clear up in a week, and the next time, I was coughing and drawing, drawing and coughing! But even though I was half dead while drawing it, the contents of the manga came out good! The frightening power of the Miura Brothers!!

This work really requires emotional strength, physical endurance, strength of nerves, and strength of concentration, so I have to be careful of my health!

Looking really happy
THAT'S A SHOT?!
FED UP
SHUUUU

First, they steamed my throat.

It's true!

I GUESSED SHE HAS A BOY-FRIEND.
SNAPP
SHE EVEN GOT BIRTHDAY AND CHRISTMAS PRESENTS, RIGHT?
ELDEST: RYUYA.
NO WAY! YOU MEAN ITO?
WITH HER, IT MIGHT NOT BE A BOY-FRIEND.
THIRD SON: TATSUYOSHI
YEAH, AND IT'S A NUISANCE JUST BEFORE DINNER!
I'M NOT SURE HOW MUCH TO COOK!
SECOND SON: YUTO.
YUTO, DO YOU THINK YOU'RE OUR MOTHER?
WHAT'S THIS DINNER TALK ABOUT?
WE ONLY HAVE ENOUGH NOODLES FOR THE FAMILY.
IF IT'S A FRIEND, I'LL HAPPILY GO OUT AND BUY MORE.
SLIS SS
IF IT'S A PUNK GUY, THEN I'LL CUT HIM INTO FILLETS.
HIS FACE LOOKS SERIOUS.
I GUESS ITO'S THAT AGE, HUH?
WHAT HAVE YOU GUYS BEEN TALKING ABOUT ALL THIS TIME?
DING DONG
THERE SHE IS!
LET'S GO !!
?!
TODAY IS THE LAST DAY OF THE YEAR.
THE "VERY IMPORTANT PERSON" I TALKED ABOUT WAS...

MAKOTO, OF COURSE!
AH!
HELLO! THANKS FOR HAVING ME OVER.
I WAS HONORED TO RECEIVE ITO'S INVITATION...
...
DON'T WASTE FORMAL GREETINGS ON THEM!
COME ON IN! COME IN!
EXCUSE ME...
BOW
AWW, MAN!! IT'S JUST MAKOTO-SAN!!
I THOUGHT IT WOULD BE A GUY!!
YOU SCARED ME WITH THOSE VAGUE WORDS!!
ha ha ha ha
HAW HAW HAW
...
BUT I AM A GUY...
IS IT OKAY FOR ME TO SUDDENLY COME OVER?
IT'S FINE! THEY'LL FORGIVE ANYTHING FOR A PRETTY GIRL.
THEY EVEN FORGIVE ME.
AS YOU CAN SEE, MY FAMILY DOESN'T KNOW THAT MAKOTO IS A GUY.
THERE'D BE TROUBLE IF THEY FOUND OUT.
THIS WAY!
IT'S BEEN A WHILE SINCE I'VE BEEN HERE.

JUST A DIGRESSION...

"Yuto" is the name of the son of our close friend Kaori. I can't believe that Kaori is a Mama! She was over to visit just the other day!

And he shares the same birthday as my sister... a Cancer, June 23. Yumi's son Ryuya shares the same birthday with me!! I love coincidences like that!!

When I was in Hokkaido, even as we went to so many places, I never could stop drawing! It's too bad the Hokkaido trip ended with just three installments! I wanted it to cover six installments, but a lot of things happened, and it didn't turn out that way. All of my new drawings for this volume are filled with Hokkaido stuff! (Is that really Hokkaido?) So, I don't have a Question Corner for this volume. Sorry! What else... Oh, yeah... I got this letter...

THE REASON I INVITED MAKOTO TO MY HOUSE IS...
EH?
YOU AREN'T GOING HOME FOR NEW YEAR'S, MAKO?
- Begin Flashback -
YEAH, EVEN IF I GO BACK, NOTHING GOOD WILL COME OF IT.
I'M GOING TO STAY IN THIS AREA ALL WINTER VACATION.
Chatter
Chatter
Chatter
BUT SHOULDN'T YOU AT LEAST GO TO WISH SEASON'S GREETINGS TO YOUR SISTERS?
IF I DO, THEN I'M PRETTY MUCH REQUIRED TO GO TO TAKAYO'S HOUSE TO GREET THEM, TOO.
THEN STAYING IN YOUR APARTMENT IS THE ONLY OPTION?
PAFF
THERE ARE SUSPICIOUS TYPES AROUND MY APARTMENT BUILDING TOO...
THOSE GUYS MY FATHER HIRES TO DO DETAILED CHECKS ON ME...
I HAVEN'T GIVEN THEM ANY DIRT TO REPORT BACK, SO RECENTLY THEY'VE BECOME EVEN MORE PERSISTENT!
I WONDER HOW MUCH HE'S PAYING THEM?
DOES THAT MEAN THAT I CAN'T COME VISIT?
YEAH... FOR A WHILE UNTIL THEY EASE UP...
BONNG

DAMMIT!! I THOUGHT FOR SURE WE'D SPEND NEW YEAR'S TOGETHER THIS YEAR!!
I REALLY DON'T WANT TO GO TO THE CLUB PARTY THIS YEAR.
HE'LL BE THERE!
I WONDER WHAT I'LL BE DOING?
WE WERE FIGHTING LAST YEAR!
TMP TMP
I'VE GOT IT!!
GRA
BB
YOU CAN COME TO MY PLACE FOR NEW YEAR'S! YOU CAN EVEN SLEEP OVER!
FOR A FEW DAYS.
IT'S A GOOD PLACE FOR YOU TO HIDE!
IT'S SO MUCH BETTER THAN BEING STUCK ALONE IN YOUR APARTMENT, RIGHT?
IT'S ALL DECIDED !!
BUT WHEN YOU SAY "SLEEP OVER"...
AFTER CLUB TODAY, GATHER YOUR STUFF AND COME OVER!
I'LL WAIT FOR YOU AT HOME!
...
- End Flashback -
AND THINGS PROCEEDED APACE.
I KIND OF FORCED HIM INTO IT.
MAKOTO CAME TO SLEEP OVER AT MY PLACE.
FOR ONCE, IT'S A GOOD THING MAKOTO'S IN DRAG.
THE GUYS WOULD SLAP ME DOWN IF THEY SAW HIM AS A MAN!
!

ONE OF THOSE MEN IS SHADOWING ME!
EH?
HE'S RIGHT THERE BEHIND THAT TELEPHONE POLE.
?!
...
WHAT'S WRONG, RYUYA?
A STRANGE MAN HAS BEEN HANGING AROUND OUR HOUSE FOR A WHILE NOW.
HE SEEMS TO BE WATCHING ITO'S ROOM.
...
HEY! THAT MEANS WE CAN'T GO OUT, HUH?
IS THIS FOR REAL?
MAYBE HE'S JUST HERE TO PUT A LITTLE PSYCHOLOGICAL PRESSURE ON ME.
HELL! I NEVER THOUGHT THEY'D COME HERE!
AH!

WOW! I'VE GOT A BRAVE BIG BROTHER!
HE DID JUST WHAT I HOPED!
THE MAN IS A FRIEND TO ALL WOMEN!
heh
...
I'D BE SO HAPPY IF THIS BUILDING COULD BECOME MAKOTO'S "SAFE HOUSE."
EVERY-BODY NEEDS...
A PLACE WHERE THEY AREN'T FORCED INTO THINGS THEY WOULD RATHER NOT DO.
HYUUUUUUUU
...A PLACE TO RELAX AND FEEL AT HOME.

Meanwhile, near the Drama Club Party...
...
COME ON!
WHAT ARE YOU DOING? GET AWAY FROM ME!
Chatter
Chatter
Chatter
FAREWELL YEAR OF THE RABBIT!
AWW... DON'T BE THAT WAY, TSUGUMI-SAN!
THIS IS OUR CHANCE TO WELCOME A BEAUTIFUL NEW YEAR TOGETHER!
I TOLD YOU I WANT NOTHING TO DO WITH YOU, YOU PERVERT!
WHAT TWISTED THAT BRAIN OF YOURS?!

STAY AWAY FROM HER HIGHNESS!
AAH!
WHO IS THAT AGAIN?
Chatter
I THINK IT'S MORITA FROM THE PHOTO CLUB.
Chatter
HE WAS DESPERATELY IN LOVE WITH TSUGUMI LAST YEAR, AND IT LOOKS LIKE IT'S STARTED AGAIN.
Can't stop some things.
See Volume 1.
WHY DO I HAVE NOTHING BUT WEIRD MEN AROUND ME?!
EVEN ITO-KUN DIDN'T COME TO THE PARTY! THIS IS THE WORST!!
SHE MAKES THEM WEIRD!
plip
plip
DID YOU CALL HER?
YES, BUT SHE ISN'T THERE!
THIS IS THE WORST PARTY EVER!!
Miura Home
IF ANYONE FROM THE CLUB CALLS, TELL THEM I'M NOT HERE!!
YEAH, OKAY.
Yuto
Ito
WELL, TSUGUMI-SAN, HOW ABOUT IT?
WILL YOU TAKE A LOOK AT "ITO MIURA REVEALED! A COLLECTION OF HIDDEN CAMERA PHOTOS: CHRISTMAS EDITION"?
heh heh heh
OH, SHUT UP! IF YOU HAD THAT...

...YOU SHOULD HAVE SAID SO RIGHT OFF THE BAT! ♡♡
ha ha
hugg
THE HOOK WAS PROPERLY BAITED.
AND AS PART OF THE PRICE, WE SHOULD SPEND NEW YEAR'S TOGETHER...
KRAKK
THOSE ARE TWO SEPARATE THINGS!!
...
BUT... IF YOU'RE THAT INTER-ESTED...
IF YOU MANAGE TO GET SOME PRIVATE PICTURES OF ITO-KUN FOR ME...
...I'LL CONSIDER GOING TO VISIT A SHRINE WITH YOU TOMORROW MORNING.
DO YOU REALLY MEAN IT, TSUGUMI-SAN?!
I WANT 24 EXPO-SURES.
THEY SHOULD BE... CASUAL PICTURES IN HER HOUSE.
RIGHT!! YOU'LL HAVE THEM!
HEY!
ha ha ha ha
ARE YOU SURE YOU WANT TO BE PROMISING STUFF LIKE THAT?!
YOU HATE HIM, DON'T YOU?
DUMMY! ITO-KUN ISN'T AT HOME!!
HO HO!
!
HOW CAN HE GET PICTURES OF HER WHEN HE DOESN'T KNOW WHERE SHE IS?!

"PRIVATE PICTURES OF ITO-KUN."
HIS NORMAL FACE ISN'T HALF BAD.
ON YOUR ORDER, I WILL TAKE MIURA...
TWI
...AND GIVE YOU THE BEST HIDDEN-CAMERA PRESENT EVER!!
TCH
HA!
THAT WOMAN HAS HUMILIATED ME IN FRONT OF TSUGUMI, AND I HOLD GRUDGES!
AH!
THIS IS MY PERFECT CHANCE FOR REVENGE!
JUST WAIT FOR THIS, TSUGUMI-SAN!!
FOLLOW HER...
...LIKE A PUPPY!
WHAT'S WRONG, ITO-SAN?
?
NOTHING. I JUST GOT A CHILL.
AM I CATCH-ING A COLD?
HEY! DON'T GO GIVING YOURSELF A FEVER, ITO. WHAT WOULD WE SAY TO DAD?
TONK
OW!
HE TREATS YOU LIKE SOME PRINCESS!
HUH?
HE DOES NOT!
NOW THAT YOU MENTION IT, WHERE IS HE?
HE HAS KARATE LESSONS, SO HE'LL BE LATE TONIGHT.
AGAIN?

And as promised...

IT WAS A MISTAKE, DAD, A MISTAKE! SEE, SHE'S A GIRL!
...
WHAT?
PLEASE FORGIVE ME. NICE TO MEET YOU, I'M ITO'S DADDY.
AAH!!
nod
I'M MAKOTO AMANO.

SHE'S A PRETTY ONE! HUH, ITO?!
HOW WONDERFUL! THE FACT THAT YOU INVITED HER OVER WITHOUT EVEN DROPPING ME A LINE... DAMN, YOU HAVE COURAGE, GIRL!!
HA HA HA HA HA HA HA HA HA HA HA HA HA
SPANK SPANK
BUT SINCE SHE'S A GIRL, I'LL FORGIVE YOU THIS TIME!
WILL YOU JUST...

...STOP SPANKING MY FANNY, YOU LOUSY, HOTHEADED OLD MAN!!
TAKE THIS! AND THIS!
I HAVE TO GIVE YOU 100 SPANKS!
UM...
...DIDN'T YOU SAY SOMETHING ABOUT A PRINCESS?
DON'T PAY ANY ATTENTION. IT'S JUST DAD'S WAY OF SHOWING AFFECTION.
RUSTLE
RUSTLE
THE PRICE OF BEING LOVED.

HE'S ALWAYS THAT WAY...
...BUT WITH ITO, HE TAKES SPECIAL PAINS TO TALK TO HER, TOO.
?

"YOU CAN'T JUDGE A PERSON'S WORTH JUST BY GRADES AND TRANSCRIPTS."

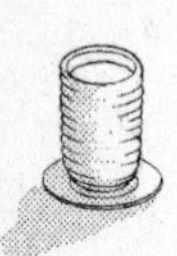

"NO MATTER HOW SMART OR GOOD-LOOKING A PERSON IS, THERE ARE GOOD PEOPLE AND BAD PEOPLE."
"IF ITO EVER BRINGS A GUY HOME, I WANT YOU TWO TO FIND OUT ABOUT HIM."

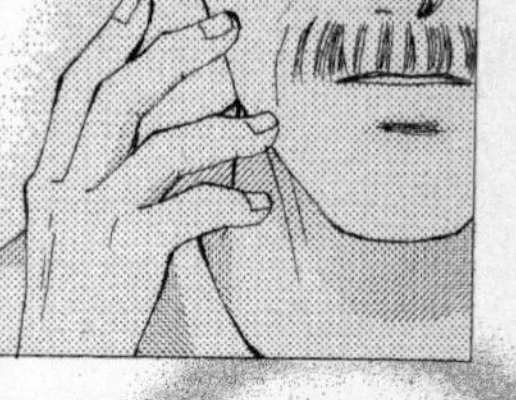
"IF A MAN LOOKS YOU IN THE EYE WHEN HE TALKS TO YOU, HE'S LIKELY TO BE SINCERE."
"IF A MAN HAS A STRONG LOOK IN HIS EYES, HE'LL USUALLY HAVE A STRONG WILL BEHIND IT."

"THAT'S THE KIND OF GUY I'D LIKE TO TAKE ITO OUT."
SO WHEN DAD DECIDES A PERSON'S WORTH, HE ALWAYS LOOKS THE MAN IN THE EYE.
WHAT'S IMPORTANT ISN'T HOW A GUY LOOKS OR DRESSES...
...BUT HIS CHARACTER! THE WAY A MAN LIVES HIS LIFE.

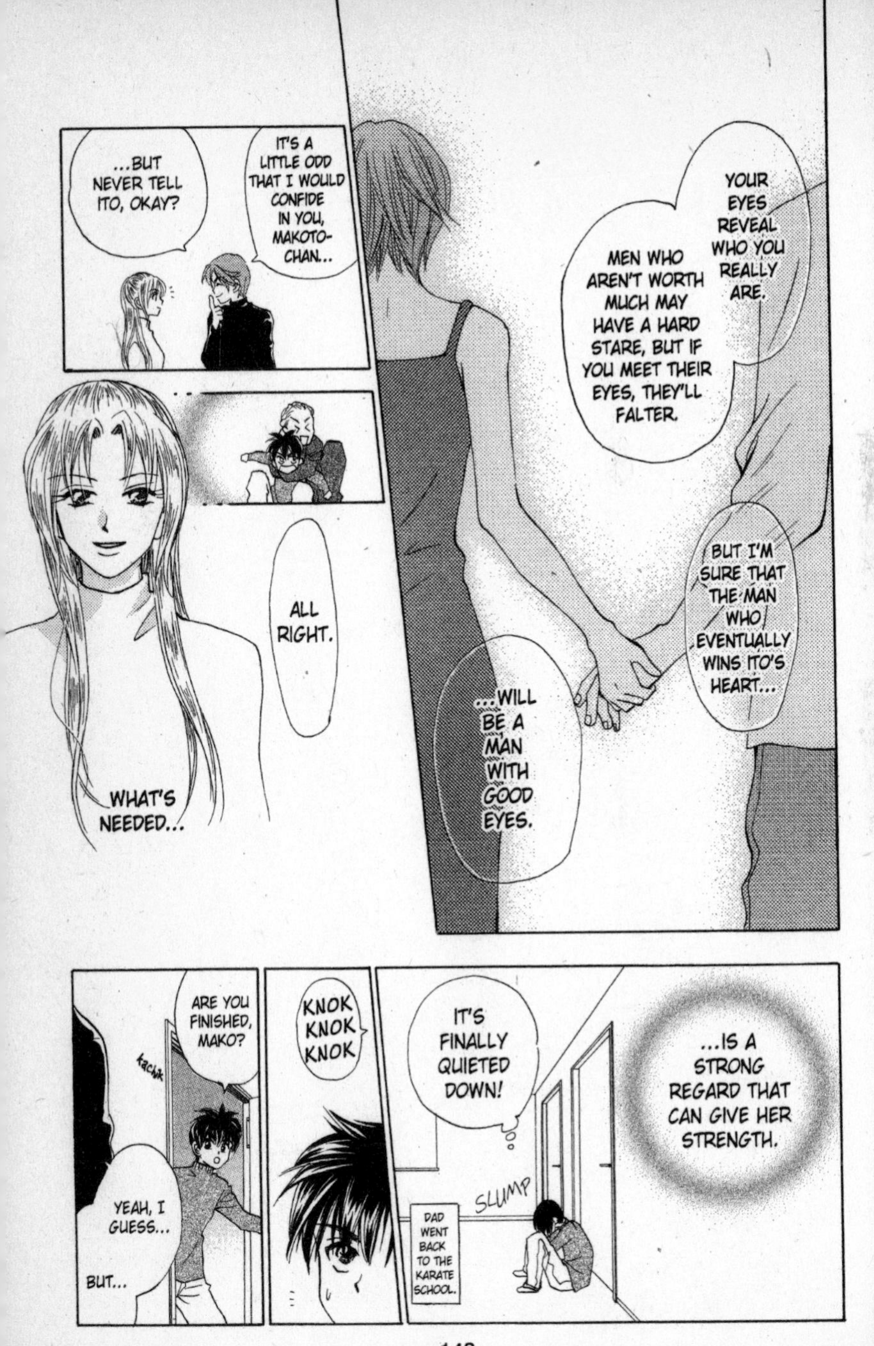
YOUR EYES REVEAL WHO YOU REALLY ARE.
MEN WHO AREN'T WORTH MUCH MAY HAVE A HARD STARE, BUT IF YOU MEET THEIR EYES, THEY'LL FALTER.
BUT I'M SURE THAT THE MAN WHO EVENTUALLY WINS ITO'S HEART...
...WILL BE A MAN WITH GOOD EYES.
IT'S A LITTLE ODD THAT I WOULD CONFIDE IN YOU, MAKOTO-CHAN...
...BUT NEVER TELL ITO, OKAY?
ALL RIGHT.
WHAT'S NEEDED...
...IS A STRONG REGARD THAT CAN GIVE HER STRENGTH.
IT'S FINALLY QUIETED DOWN!
SLUMP
DAD WENT BACK TO THE KARATE SCHOOL.
KNOK KNOK KNOK
ARE YOU FINISHED, MAKO?
kachak
YEAH, I GUESS...
BUT...

...
...IS IT REALLY OKAY TO GO AROUND DRESSED LIKE THIS?
Ito's→ clothes.
IT'S JUST FINE! I WANT YOU TO FEEL RELAXED.
AS LONG AS I LOCK THE DOOR, NOBODY'LL COME IN.
EVERYTHING'S FINE.
KACHAK
EH?
UM, ITO-SAN. MAYBE YOU SHOULDN'T LOCK THE DOOR.
?
WHY NOT? IT'S SAFER, ISN'T IT?
...
IT'S A LITTLE DISAPPOINTING THAT SHE TRUSTS ME SO MUCH.
RUSTLE RUSTLE
I'M SO GLAD THAT WE LEFT THE CLUB EARLY!
Getting comfortable...
...
Sleepy...
SOMEHOW...
...I FEEL I CAN RELAX IN THIS ROOM.
EH? REALLY?
...
IT HAS YOUR SMELL, ITO-SAN.

...
HE'S ASLEEP ALREADY.
ZZZZ ZZZZ
NEXT YEAR'S NEW YEAR'S, AND EACH ONE AFTER...
...IT'D BE NICE IF I COULD SPEND THEM WITH MAKOTO.
I'VE FINALLY FOUND MIURA'S HOUSE!
NOW IT'S TIME FOR THE PHOTO SESSION!
Morita
HAH HAH HAH
PRESIDENT MORITA...
ARE YOU REALLY GOING TO DO THIS?

OF COURSE!! THIS IS THE WISH OF TSUGUMI-SAN!!
LET'S NOT, OKAY? IT'S AGAINST THE LAW!
IF WE HAVE TO, LET'S DO IT DURING DAYTIME.
Battlefield Costume
I LOVE TSUGUMI
WHAT TALK IS THIS?!
I'M GOING TO GET MY PHOTOS FAIRLY!!
SHF
IT IS AN ORDER FROM THE GODDESS I AM FATED TO WORSHIP!
PRES-IDENT MORITA!
GODDESS?!
huh?
AH! OH, NO!
I DOZED OFF WITHOUT REALIZING IT!
OH, MAN!
IT'S 7:00 ALREADY?
HE'S FAST ASLEEP!
SO HE CAN SLEEP AT MY PLACE WITH NO PROBLEM!
ZZZZZZZ
"THERE ARE SUSPICIOUS TYPES AROUND MY APARTMENT."
...
...
I'LL JUST LET HIM SLEEP.
SHFF SHFF

TMP TMP
GOTTA HIT THE TOILET!
HEH!
THIS MUST BE ITO'S ROOM!
SST
OH, ITO. WE'LL HAVE NOODLES IN 10 MINUTES.
TUMP
OKAY!
TUMP
TUMP
FIRST, I'LL TAKE A FEW OF THE ROOM.
HM?
MMM...
ITO-SAN ISN'T HERE.
huh?
?!
IS THAT MIURA'S BOY-FRIEND?
TH-THEN...
SHF
...THIS IS A WORLD-CLASS SCOOP!!
FA
SSH

BAMM
THAT'S A CAMERA FLASH!
?!
...
WH--

DOKAMM
WHO THE HELL ARE YOU?!
?!
EH? IT COULDN'T BE...
BAM
BAM
MAKOTO?!
WHAT WAS THAT?
IT CAME FROM ITO'S ROOM!
!!
THERE'S A WEIRD MAN IN ITO'S ROOM?!
IT'S THE WEIRDO FROM THIS AFTERNOON! I'M SURE OF IT!
HE'S AFTER ITO! DAMMIT!!
HE EVEN TOOK A PICTURE!
WHAAAT?!
WE'LL KILL HIM AND COOK HIM.
YÛTO!!
OH!
THERE HE IS!
HE'S ON THE ROOF!
I DON'T BELIEVE IT! NO MATTER HOW GOOD MAKOTO IS...
...ALL THREE OF MY BROTHERS KNOW KARATE, SO THERE'S NO WAY HE CAN GET AWAY!

I CAN'T WIN! HOW DID THIS HAPPEN?
SHF
THERE WAS SOMEONE ELSE!
HE'S PROBABLY STILL ON THE GROUNDS!
TMP
KAK KAK
KAK KAK
KAK
KAK KAK
!
HE'S FAST!
WHAT'S WITH THAT GUY?! HE'S BLOCKING ALL OF RYUYA'S ATTACKS!
AARG! HE'S GOING TO BE FOUND OUT THIS WAY!

WHOOSH
I LOVE TSUGUMI
...
GIVE UP AND LET ME CATCH YOU!!
!!
SHS SHS SHS SHS SHS SHS SHS
KRAKK KRAKK

SHS SHS
HE FELL!
THAT LAST TIME... DID YOU HIT HIM?
...
IT WAS SO DARK, IT WAS HARD TO TELL.
THAT'S THE GARDEN BELOW, RIGHT?
ANYWAY, LET'S GO GET HIM.
YEAH...
...!!
I DON'T BELIEVE IT! HE DIDN'T FALL NORMALLY...
HE'S PRETTY SHREWD. MAYBE HE GOT AWAY.
IF HIS SECRET WERE TO GET OUT...
THERE HE IS!
HE'S PASSED OUT!
IF HE WERE CAUGHT HERE...
HUH? THIS GUY'S JUST A HIGH SCHOOL KID!
FWUMP
ANYWAY, LET'S CALL THE POLICE.
AND FIND OUT WHO HE IS!
B-BMP
"MY WISH IS..."

"...TO GRADUATE SAFELY FROM HIGH SCHOOL...
"...AND TO LIVE SIDE-BY-SIDE WITH THE WOMAN I LOVE."
NO!!
WAIT--
HYUUUUUU
...
WHO'S THIS?
HUH?

WE DON'T KNOW. THAT'S WHY WE HAVE TO FIND OUT.
WHAT A PAIN!
RIGHT! THAT TAKES CARE OF THE NEGA-TIVES!

?!?
EH? RYUYA, IT LOOKS LIKE YOU DID HIT HIM AFTER ALL.
LOOK AT THE BUMPS.
HE'S GOT BLEACHED HAIR...
IT LOOKED BLONDE BEFORE...
IT'S SO DARK.

OH, ITO! IS MAKOTO-CHAN ALL RIGHT?
I HAVEN'T SEEN HER.
THAT'S WHAT I WANT TO KNOW!
HA HA HA
UM...

THERE ARE TWO GUYS HANGING AROUND OUTSIDE THE FRONT GATE.
THEY SAY THEY HAVE AN ERRAND THERE, BUT...
OH, MAKOTO-CHAN! WHERE HAVE YOU BEEN?
HA HA HA
I WENT OUT TO MAKE A CALL ON MY CEL PHONE.
YOU...
...?!
nod
That was fast, Mako!
SORRY IF I WAS A BOTHER.

HE'LL *NEVER* GO NEAR YOUR SISTER AGAIN!
YOU BETTER BELIEVE HE WON'T! OR NEXT TIME WE'LL HAVE HIM ARRESTED FOR STALKING!
heeeee
I *KNEW* THIS'D HAPPEN!
YES, SIR! THANK YOU FOR BEING SO LENIENT!
...
THAT WAS SAKURA HIGH'S PHOTO CLUB?
Yuto
SMALL WORLD.
ROUGH CLUB TO BE IN.
POOR CLUB MEMBERS.

WHERE'S ITO?
EATING TOSHI-KOSHI NOODLES IN HER ROOM WITH MAKOTO-CHAN.
RYUYA, YOU LOOKED SCARY TONIGHT!
heh
DON'T SAY THAT UNTIL YOU LOOK IN THE MIRROR!
WELL...
...I'M GLAD THAT ITO'S SAFE ANYWAY.
THANK GOD DAD WASN'T HOME FOR THIS!
YEAH...
LIKE I SAID, I FELL OFF OF THE ROOF ON PURPOSE.
I SAW MORITA TRYING TO GET AWAY.
ONCE I WAS ON THE GROUND, I CAUGHT HIM, PUT HIM UNDER, AND MADE THE SWITCH.
I DIDN'T HAVE TIME TO LET YOU IN ON THE PLAN.
SORRY IF IT CAUSED YOU ANY WORRIES.
...
TONK
Don't drink it!

IS THAT HOW IT WORKED?
WELL, I...
YOU FELL SO CONVINCINGLY! I WAS COMPLETELY FOOLED!
BAM
SORRY! SORRY!
I DON'T GET BEATEN THAT EASILY.
I THOUGHT THE WHOLE JIG WAS UP FOR YOU!
AND MY FAMILY'S TO BLAME, TOO!
I DO TOO, THOUGH...
ANYTHING SLIGHTLY OUT OF THE ORDINARY, AND THEY GO TO BATTLE!
THAT ISN'T TRUE!
Ryuya sprayed Makoto with water the first time they met.
THEY'RE JUST LOOKING OUT FOR THEIR SISTER'S INTERESTS.
...YOUR BROTHER CHASED HIM OFF FOR YOUR SAKE!
I DON'T BUY IT.
YOU'RE SO CUTE!
FOR EXAMPLE, THAT GUY TAILING ME THIS AFTER-NOON...

HE WAS WATCHING ME, BUT THEY THOUGHT HE WAS STALKING YOU, RIGHT?
REMEM-BER THAT SMILE HE GAVE YOU AFTER-WARDS?
IT ISN'T THE WAY PEOPLE TALK THAT SAYS THE MOST ABOUT THEM.
REALLY, EVERYBODY LOVES YOU!
9 years old
9 years old
4 years old
2 years old
IT'S HARD TO CHANGE THE LOVE FAMILY MEMBERS HAVE FOR EACH OTHER.
TO ME, THIS IS THE IDEAL HOUSEHOLD.
I'D HAVE LIKED TO HAVE BROTHERS.

...

STRANGELY...

...I WAS ABLE TO ACCEPT MAKOTO'S WORDS WITHOUT PUTTING UP A FUSS.
YEAH, OKAY.

ITO, THE COUNT-DOWN'S STARTED!
KACHIK
OKAY, WE'RE COMING DOWN!
THAT WAS CLOSE!...
...

MAKOTO REALLY IS...
...AN IRREPLACEABLE PART OF MY LIFE.
5. 4. 3. 2. 1!!

I LIKE SPENDING TIME ALONE WITH HIM, BUT...
EVERYBODY SEEMS SO HAPPY.
...TIMES LIKE THIS ARE BETTER WITH A LOT OF PEOPLE.
HAPPY NEW YEAR!!

I GUESS I HAVE ANOTHER ASSIGNMENT TO WORK ON THIS YEAR...
A STRONG LOOK IN THE EYE.
HUH?
NOTHING. JUST TALKING TO MYSELF.

JANG
JANG
JANG
OH... WHOOAAAA!
CHATTER
LOOK AT ALL THE PEOPLE!
CHATTER
THERE MAY BE PEOPLE WE KNOW HERE, HUH?

-Behind the Scenes Story- ⑥

That thing that Toki-chan talks about is an actual real-world story. A way to get rid of bad luck If you get "bad luck" from a shrine fortune, be sure to tie it backwards on the shrine tree branches. The very year I was supposed to take my high school exams, I got a "bad luck" fortune at New Year's! Of course, I still passed my exams!! Banzai! If I weren't able to go to that high school, I probably wouldn't be drawing manga right now. Also, don't go picking up any money from the shrine grounds! If you pick up money, you're also picking up other people's bad luck! (Try it! Drop a 500-yen piece on the ground at the shrine.)

This has been a warning!

HUH?

I wonder what future the other one told of?

When I got the bad-luck fortune, two fortunes came out of the box at once.

COTTON CANDY
NEW YEAR'S...
MAKO! I WANT COTTON CANDY! COTTON CANDY!!
WE'LL GET SOME LATER!
WE CAME TO THE SHRINE TO PROPERLY SEE IN THE NEW YEAR.

AFTER WE BEAT MY BROTHERS SILLY AT IROHA...
YOU CAN'T RUN UNTIL WE GET EVEN!!
SCAMPER
WE DECIDED TO TAKE THE LONG COMMUTE TO A REALLY BIG SHRINE.
I DIDN'T GET ENOUGH SLEEP!
WE PLAYED NEW YEAR'S GAMES UNTIL LATE INTO THE NIGHT.
TMP TMP TMP TMP
KYAAAAA
BUMP
WHONK
ITO-SAN, ARE YOU ALL RIGHT?
THOSE LITTLE BRATS!
I WAS OFF MY GUARD FOR AN INSTANT!
SOME-HOW...
...I'VE HAD BAD LUCK EVER SINCE I LEFT HOME.
GLOOP
AH!
A HUGE SWEET-BEAN PASTE STAIN!
HUH?
I LOST THE MONEY I WAS GOING TO USE FOR THE OFFERING!
EH?

I HAVEN'T DONE ANYTHING, BUT BAD THINGS KEEP PILING ON!
A RASH OF BAD LUCK THE FIRST THING IN THE NEW YEAR!
JANG
JANG
Borrowed a coin from Makoto. (Five-yen piece)
THAT TOOK YOU A WHILE, ITO-SAN.
chatter
chatter
I HAVE A LOT TO WISH FOR.
AND PLEASE LET MAKOTO GET THROUGH THE YEAR SAFELY.
chatter
AND...
KA CHANK
...THIS YEAR, PLEASE LET ME BE SOMEONE...
...WHO LOOKS GOOD ON MAKOTO'S ARM.
...
THE BELLS BROKE AND CRASHED TO THE GROUND!
WHAT ?!
I'VE NEVER SEEN THAT BEFORE!
OKAY, THAT SHOULD BE ENOUGH WISHING.

おみくじ
FORTUNE
凶
BAD LUCK
WISH: WILL BE DIFFICULT TO SEE COME TRUE.
HEALTH: IF YOU CATCH A COLD, IT WILL TAKE AN UNUSUALLY LONG TIME TO CURE.
WORK: A BIG PROBLEM AWAITS YOU.
PREGNANCY: BEWARE OF A DIFFICULT DELIVERY.
MONEY MATTERS:
LOVE:
ALL OF THIS MAY BE AN OMEN OF WHAT'S TO COME.

YUP! BAD LUCK IS FOLLOWING ME AROUND!
...
GREAT LUCK
DOOOM
BUT THIS MAY MEAN THAT YOU HAVE **STRONG** LUCK!
YOU GOT THE FORTUNE WITH THE LEAST PERCENTAGE CHANCE!
POIT
YOU GOT "GREAT LUCK," SO I DON'T WANT TO HEAR ABOUT IT FROM YOU!
shp

VWMM
WHAT'S THIS, IKKO? YOU GOT THE BAD-LUCK FORTUNE?
?!?
ZWATCH
YO. HAPPY NEW YEAR.
IT'S QUITE A COINCIDENCE TO MEET YOU HERE.

IT'S MIURA.
AND MAKOTO-SAN, TOO!
Chatter
Chatter
THIS IS AN EXTENSION OF THE NEW YEAR'S PARTY.
WE ALL DECIDED TO VISIT THE SHRINE TOGETHER.
WHY DO I HAVE TO MEET HIM THIS EARLY IN THE NEW YEAR?
WHAT'S WITH THEM?
YOU DON'T HAVE TO PUT YOUR GUARD UP.
I AIN'T DOING ANYTHING.
FWIKK
HERE, LOOK.
?
KRIP KRIP
IF YOU GET A BAD FORTUNE, YOU DO THIS.
YOU TIE THE FORTUNE WITH YOUR LEFT HAND, AND THE BAD LUCK DISAPPEARS.
EH?
?!
PWIK
IT'S AN OLD TRADITION.
A WAY TO WARD OFF EVIL.
IF THAT'S YOUR THING, GIVE IT A TRY.
...

I'M SURPRISED TOKI-CHAN WENT OFF LIKE THAT.
I THOUGHT HE'D BE MORE PERSIS-TENT.
...
I'LL DO IT RIGHT AWAY.
SHF SHF
DON'T SAY THINGS LIKE THAT. YOU MIGHT LET YOUR GUARD DOWN AGAIN.
I WON'T! I MEAN, LOOK!
I HEARD THAT TOKI-CHAN HAS *THREE* GIRLFRIENDS NOW!
HEARD IT AT CHRISTMAS!
I THINK HE'S FINALLY GIVEN UP ON ME!

I'LL BET A HUNDRED MILLION YEN THAT SHE GETS FOOLED AGAIN.
A 100 MILLION ?!
ANYWAY, I'VE DECIDED THAT HE'S THE ENEMY.
WE CAN'T TRUST HIM!
...

BESIDES, THOSE ARE PROBABLY GIRLFRIENDS FOR CHRISTMAS USE ONLY.
WOW, HE'S HARSH!
tmp
tmp
AS EVER, WHEN IT COMES TO TOKI-CHAN, MAKOTO'S MOOD DETERIORATES.
KYAA!
KYAA!
WHERE'S TSUGUMI-SEMPAI?
SHE DECIDED TO DO SOMETHING ELSE.
THANK GOD!
YOSHIRO, I BOUGHT ENOUGH GOOD-HEALTH PRAYERS AND PROTECTION CHARMS FOR EVERYBODY.
FOR THE PEOPLE WHO DIDN'T COME, TOO.
EH?
IT'S BEST IF THE WHOLE CLUB HAS THE SAME TYPE.

OF COURSE IT'LL ALL BE ON MY TAB!! MY OTOSHIDAMA CAME IN!
WOW!
KYAA!
ALL RIGHT!
THAT'S GREAT!!
EVERYBODY'S GOTTA EAT SOME HACHIFUKU-MOCHI!
BY WHICH I MEAN THAT I'M HUNGRY FOR IT.
IF YOU LOOK BEYOND THE WAY HE IS WITH WOMEN...
HE'S ACTUALLY A NICE, FUNNY GUY.
KIND OF A BRUTE, BUT...
KYA HA HA HA
He likes NOBUKO.
I'LL GO WASH UP.
I DON'T WANT MOCHI.
OKAY.
IKKO, YOSHIRO WILL NEVER BE ABLE TO CARRY ALL OF THAT STUFF HIMSELF. GO HELP HIM!
THE STALL'S THROUGH THE SHRINE GATE AND TO YOUR RIGHT.
TMP
!
I'M ON IT!
SHSH SHSH SHSH
THAT'S THE GATE THERE, RIGHT?
THE SHRINE GROUNDS HERE ARE HUGE!!

...

HUH?

WHAT'S GOING ON?
THERE AREN'T ANY STALLS HERE...
HEY! YOSHIRO!!
POFF

GRIN
FINALLY, WE'RE ALONE! ♪

?!
YOSHIRO WENT ONE BLOCK OVER THAT WAY.
WHOOSH
I'M SURPRISED HOW STRONG MAKOTO-CHAN'S GUARD IS. I COULDN'T GET CLOSE!
!

It looks like I've come to the point where I'm not able to answer your letters! Before, I used to separate it out into Summer and Winter and mail out replies on postcards, but recently that's become more and more of a problem! But I still read every letter sent to me! I don't skip one word! It's one of the few things that really cheers me up! It keeps me going! Thank you all. I really appreciate it!

So, now I'd like to answer a question that has come up a lot recently. I was going to answer this only after I'd become an award-winning artist, but this past March and April, the question has come up time and time again. "How old are you?" Well, I'm not really trying to hide my age! Last March, I turned 22 years old. A pair of deuces!

By the way, this May will mark the fourth anniversary since my debut. How time flies! This fall will see the third anniversary of W-Juliet! I was 19 when it started! So young! And that draws Volume 4 to a close. Let's meet again in Volume 5, okay?

Sorry my writing is so messy! I wrote these 1/4-page columns on the train!

WAIT A MINUTE! I THOUGHT YOU HAD FINALLY GIVEN UP ON ME!
WHEN DID I EVER SAY ANYTHING LIKE THAT?
ANY-WAY...
...WE'LL PUT OFF THE BOYFRIEND/GIRLFRIEND TALK FOR NOW...
HMMMM
WHAT I WANT IS TO MAKE UP FOR YOUR MISSING THE YEAR-END PARTY BY HAVING YOU HANG OUT WITH ME.

HE HASN'T CHANGED A BIT!!
GONNG
A HUNDRED MILLION.
YAAY
YAAY
chatter
chatter
chatter
chatter
I THINK SHE WENT TO HELP YOSHIRO BRING THE FOOD.
RIGHT!
HEY, THEY'RE BACK!
HUH?
WHERE'S ITO-SAN?

I HAVE RETURNED BEARING GIFTS!
COULD SOMEBODY LEND ME A HAND?
YO-SHIRO!
CHATTER
HEY! INCREDIBLE! 60 OF THEM?
CHATTER
...??
YOSHIRO, WHERE'S ITO-SAN?
? BEATS ME.
I'D LIKE TO KNOW WHERE TOKI-SEMPAI IS.
...
MAKOTO-SAN SURE IS FAST.
YEAH...
REALLY FAST.
hyuuuuuu
"WE CAN'T TRUST HIM!"
HOW MANY TIMES DO I HAVE TO SAY IT?
TMP

I ALREADY SAID!!
TMP
TMP
TMP
TMP
I TURN YOU DOWN EVERY SINGLE TIME! WHY DO YOU HAVE TO BE SO BULL HEADED!
PERSIST-ENCE IS IN MY NATURE!
TMP
TMP
COME! FLY INTO MY WAITING ARMS!
CUT THE CRAP!
WHAT'S SO GREAT ABOUT ME?!
I TOLD YOU BEFORE! I WANT TO MOLD YOU!
I EVEN LIKE THE SOUND OF THOSE WORDS!
?!

I WANT TO TAME YOU!
heh heh heh heh
SHUSH
SHUSH
SHUSH
SHUSH
NEVER! ABSOLUTELY NOT!!
!!
OH, NO! SOMEBODY'S THERE!!
ZZLIPP
!
WHUMPH
heh
IT SEEMS TO ME THE FIRST TIME WE MET...
...THE VERY SAME THING HAPPENED.

ARE YOU ALL RIGHT?
...!!
THUMP
LONG TIME, NO SEE, MIURA-CHAN.
I THOUGHT THAT WAS YOU I SAW.
AND NOW, HERE YOU ARE.
YES!
HE'S THAT GUY FROM HOKKAIDO!
SHF
IKKO!
YOU KNOW HIM?
LET GO!
OH. YEAH...
WE MET ON THE CLASS TRIP TO HOKKAIDO.
BUT I THOUGHT YOU *LIVED* IN HOKKAIDO!
ORIGINALLY, I'M FROM CHIBA.
LAST MONTH, I MOVED TO NAGOYA.
!

THAT BOY!
HE'S FROM THE SCHOOL TRIP!!

YUTAKA SAKAMOTO. 17 YEARS OLD.
185 CM (6' 1"), 78 KG (172 LBS), A SPRINTER FOR THE TRACK AND FIELD CLUB, I'VE BEEN TO PREFECTURAL FINALS THREE TIMES.
MY SPECIAL TALENT IS EATING RAMEN NOODLES THROUGH MY NOSE.
REMEMBER ME, OKAY?

RAMEN THOUGH HIS NOSE?
BUT WHAT ARE YOU DOING HERE?
YOU SAID YOU MOVED TO NA-GOYA...
OH, THAT ...

STARTING IN JANUARY, I'LL BE TRANSFERRING INTO SAKURA HIGH!
GRIN

IT TOOK A LONG TIME FOR MY FATHER TO SEE IT MY WAY...
...BUT IT HAPPENED, SO I HOPE TO SEE A LOT OF YOU. ♡

YOU SAID YOU ALWAYS GO TO BOYS' SCHOOLS!
TMP
BUT MIURA-CHAN, REMEMBER THAT TIME...
...WHEN YOU YELLED AT ME?
"YOU SHOULD TRY TO FIND A WAY OUT OF YOUR SITUATION."

I DOUBT THAT THERE'S ANY OTHER GIRL IN THE WORLD WHO WOULD GIVE ME A GOOD KICK IN THE PANTS LIKE THAT!
IT SAVED MY LIFE!
...
HA HA HA
THAT'S WHEN I DECIDED ON SAKURA HIGH, WHERE *YOU* ARE!
...

HE'S TRANS-FERRING ?!
HA HA HA HA
THIS IS THE FIRST TIME I'VE REGRETTED WHAT I SAID TO MOTIVATE SOMEBODY!
DAMMIT! THAT GUY'S SEEN ME AS A MAN!
I CAN'T JUST BURST OUT INTO THE OPEN.
I'VE BEEN WATCHING YOU TWO FOR A WHILE...
...AND HERE'S THE THING...
?
MIURA-CHAN CAME OUT AND RE-JECTED YOU.
WHY DON'T YOU BE A MAN AND JUST LET IT GO?
I DON'T KNOW WHO YOU ARE, BUT...
HUH?

INTERESTING! REMEMBER THIS, BRAT! PEOPLE IN THIS TOWN EITHER RECALL MY NAME WITH FONDNESS OR THEY REGRET IT!
EH?
SOUNDS LIKE FUN! LET'S MIX IT UP!
YOU'RE THE ONE WHO'S OUT OF PLACE HERE!
DOOM
DOOM
DOOM

WHOOSH
ALL YOU HAVE TO KNOW IS THAT SHE IS MINE!! HOW I TREAT HER IS UP TO ME!!
WH--
!
HUH?
WHAT ARE YOU SAYING ABOUT *MY* GIRL-FRIEND?!
YOU'RE THE ONE WHO'S OUT OF PLACE! GET OUT!
WHO THE HELL ARE YOU?!
GRABB
OW...
WHO DO YOU THINK YOU ARE, YOU SNIVELING LITTLE BRAT! LET GO!
YOU LET GO, YOU DROOPY-EYED IDIOT!
WELL, YOU'RE DROOPY-EYED, TOO!
...
GRRRRR
OW! OW! OW! OW!

WHAT'S GOING ON WITH THESE CLUELESS JERKS?!
IF THIS ISN'T BAD LUCK, I DON'T KNOW WHAT IS!
FWAFF

MA-KOTO?!
!
TUMP
MAKOTO-CHA--
?
YOU'RE FORCING YOUR FEELINGS ONTO HER...
...WITHOUT CARING WHETHER SHE RETURNS THE FEELING!
YOU TOO, TOKI-SEMPAI.
IF YOU KNOW ITO-SAN SO WELL, YOU SHOULD KNOW THAT FORCE WOULDN'T MAKE HER LIKE YOU.
PEOPLE WHO DON'T SPARE A THOUGHT FOR THEIR PARTNERS...
...AREN'T ABLE TO REALLY LOVE ANYBODY!
SHE'S...
...NOT A *TOY* FOR YOU TO PLAY WITH!

HMMMMM
HMMMMM
SHE SEEMED A LOT LIKE THAT GUY.
...
NAWW!
FOR GOD'S SAKE!
HOW MANY TIMES DO I HAVE TO RESCUE YOU BEFORE YOU'RE SATISFIED?
THANK YOU, MAKO!
I'M SORRY THIS HAPPENED SO EARLY IN THE NEW YEAR.
CHATTER
CHATTER
CHATTER
YOU OWE ME A 100 MILLION YEN.
Cotton Candy
EHHH ?!
...
I'M JUST A BAD LUCK CHARM!
SAKAMOTO SAYS HE'LL BE TRANSFERRING TO OUR SCHOOL IN THE THIRD TERM.
AWW! I REALLY HAVE THIS AWFUL PREMONITION!

LUCKY
GREAT LUCK
GOOD LUCK
NOT MUCH LUCK
NO LUCK
BAD LUCK
UNLUCKY
LOOK. YOUR FORTUNE SAID YOU'LL HAVE BAD LUCK, AND THAT'S AS BAD AS FORTUNES CAN GET. SO NOW YOU'VE SEEN THE WORST.
FROM HERE ON OUT, IT CAN ONLY GET BETTER.
I DON'T KNOW...
BE-SIDES...
FLIP
IF YOU AVERAGE YOURS OUT WITH MINE, IT'LL PROBABLY COME OUT SOMEWHERE IN THE "GOOD LUCK" RANGE.
...IT WAS TOO SOON TO RELAX YET.
IN THE FUTURE WE'LL BE DOING THIS TOGETHER ANYWAY.
WAIT A MINUTE! HALFWAY BETWEEN US IS "NOT MUCH LUCK."
"GREAT LUCK" HAS A LOT OF POWER SO IT SKEWS THE AVERAGE.
BUT...
EH?

HEY, WE DON'T HAVE A CHOICE, DO WE?
YOU INVITED MAKOTO-SAN OVER AT THE LAST MINUTE!
WE DIDN'T HAVE TIME TO MAKE HER BED!
IT'LL BE NIGHTTIME BEFORE WE FIND A FUTON IN THERE!
WHAT DID YOU GUYS **DO** ALL DAY?
WE DRANK SAKE AND SLEPT.
YOU HAD ALL DAY!
BAM
WHO CARES? YOU'RE BOTH GIRLS!
IT MIGHT BE A LITTLE COZY...
...BUT NOTHING'S GOING TO HAPPEN IF YOU SLEEP TOGETHER!
NOW THAT HE MENTIONS IT, LAST NIGHT WE WERE ALL HAVING FUN...
...
...STAYING UP, PLAYING GAMES IN THE LIVING ROOM.

WHEN WE SLEEP TONIGHT, IT'LL BE IN THE SAME ROOM!
DO DOOOOM

WHEN YOU SAID WE'D BE TO-GETHER...
...I DIDN'T EXPECT IT TO MEAN THE BED.
HA HA HA!
...
Uncomfortable
glance

KLAP
ALL RIGHT.
I'LL SLEEP UNDER THE KOTATSU, YOU TAKE THE BED.
WHAT ARE YOU SAYING? IT'S YOUR BED, ITO-SAN, YOU SLEEP THERE!
IT'S ALL RIGHT! YOU'RE THE GUEST HERE!
IT'S NOT ALL RIGHT! YOU'RE THE GIRL! YOU'LL GET A COLD ON THE FLOOR!
GENDER HAS NOTHING TO DO WITH IT!
IT'S MY ROOM, AND I'LL TAKE THE KOTATSU!
MAKO, THE BED IS YOURS! USE IT!!
YOU TAKE THE BED, ITO-SAN!
I REFUSE TO ACCEPT IT!

HUSHHHHHHHHHHH
...
...
HE'S A LITTLE SCARY.

...
IF YOU'RE GOING TO USE THE KOTATSU, MAKO, THEN I'LL BE RIGHT THERE SLEEPING BESIDE YOU!
THAT'S FINE WITH YOU, RIGHT?
...
...

RUSTLE RUSTLE
I WON!
BUT SOMETHING'S NOT RIGHT.
IT'S LIKE HE BACKED DOWN TOO EASILY.
IT'S JUST DIFFERENT BETWEEN AN AFTERNOON NAP AND SLEEPING AT NIGHT.
Afternoon nap.
AAH-CHOO!
DIDN'T I TELL YOU?
IT WASN'T BECAUSE I WAS COLD!

...
I'M HAPPY THAT YOU ARE WORRIED ABOUT MY COMFORT, BUT...
TRY TO UNDER-STAND THAT.
...ON MY LIST, ITO-SAN, YOU COME FIRST.
...
ZZZZZZZ

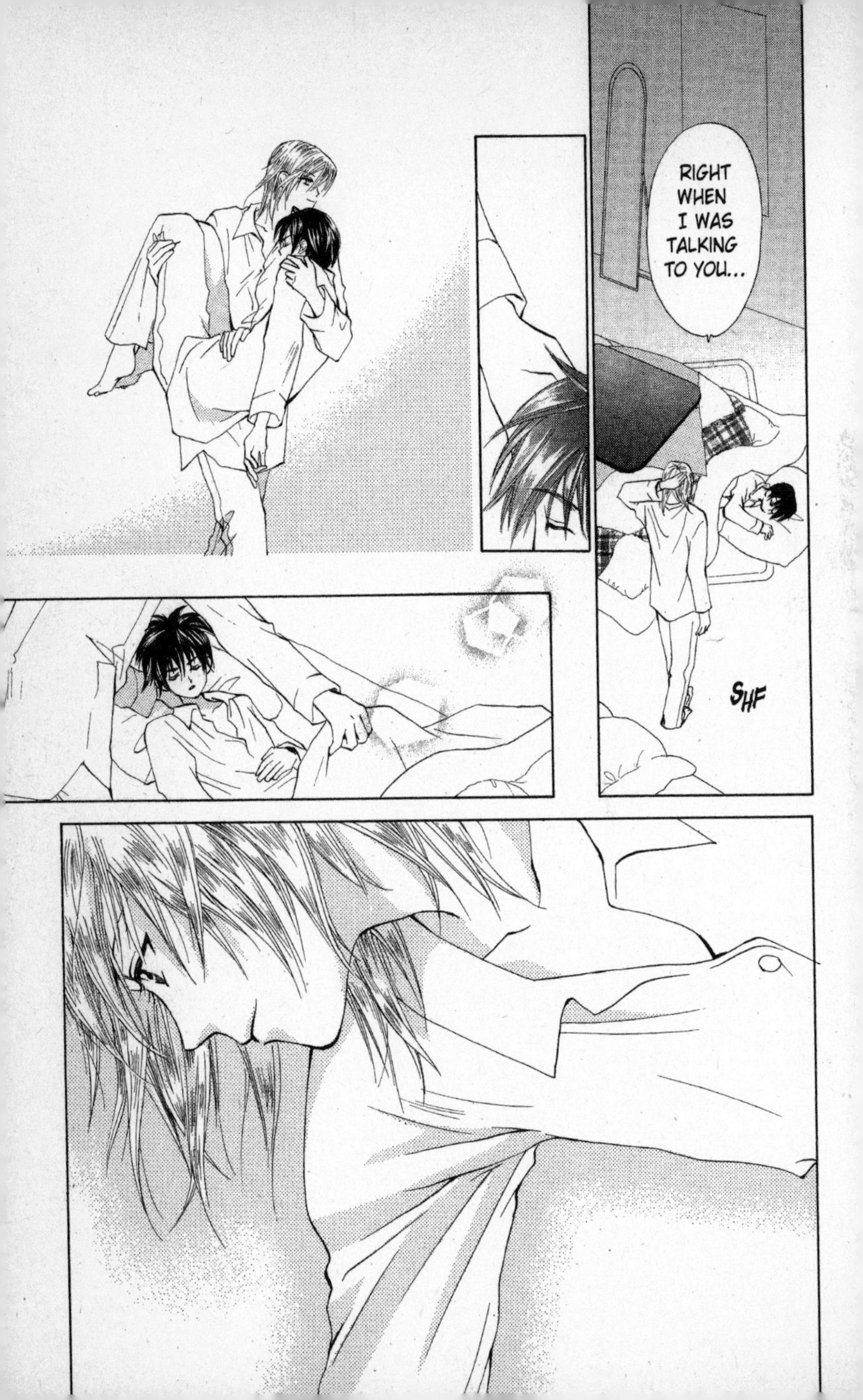
RIGHT WHEN I WAS TALKING TO YOU...
SHF

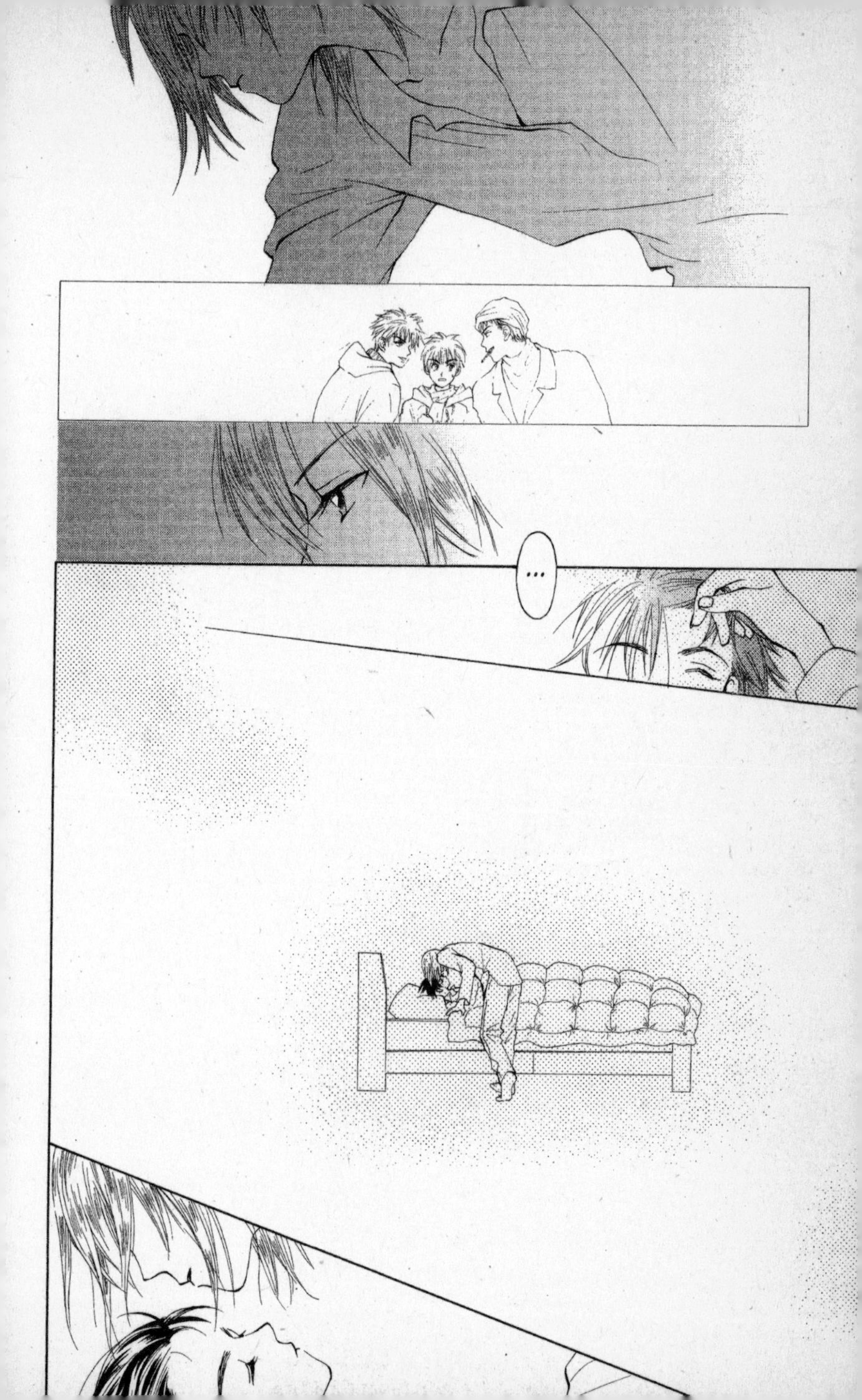

I WON'T LOSE!
I DON'T CARE WHAT GUY COMES ALONG!
I'M NOT GOING TO HAND YOU OVER.
I'M GOING TO PROTECT YOU.

...
VERY EARLY IN THE NEW YEAR...
...A BUNCH OF STUPID THINGS HAPPENED...
...
DAMMIT! NOW I CAN'T SLEEP!
...BUT PLEASE LET US SPEND *THIS* YEAR IN HAPPINESS.

THE VOLUME-ENDING AFTERWORD MANGA!
Behind the Scenes
UM... A LOT OF LETTERS ASKED ME TO SHOW ITO IN A KIMONO THIS VOLUME. SO I DECIDED TO TRY IT OUT.
WITH ALL THESE REQUESTS, IT'S LIKE THE OPENING OF A HUGE COMPETITION.
THE MOST REQUESTS.
HANG IN THERE, MAKO-RIN!
SHE'S MINE !!

ONE MORE SCHOOL EXCURSION

With the W-J Char-acters

AS A SUDDEN CHANGE OF PACE, I'M GOING TO WRITE ABOUT A DREAM I HAD WHILE DOING THE SCHOOL EXCURSION STORIES.

WHAT A HUGE HOTEL!

THIS IS REALLY RITZY!

RUMOR HAS IT THAT THEY HAVE GREAT HOT SPRINGS BATHS WITH FISH DINNERS COOKED TO PER-FECTION!
THEY EVEN HAVE A NICE POOL!
TROMP TROMP
Loves fish
THIS IS GONNA BE SO MUCH FUN!
MEN'S BATHS

For some reason we could see everything.

HOT SPRINGS BATHS AND FISH...
FISH...
FISH?!

I TRIED TO PRETEND THAT I NEVER SAW.
THERE WERE PEOPLE INSIDE!
IT'S SOME KIND OF HOTEL UNIFORM!
AFTER THAT, NOBODY EVEN TRIED TO BRING UP THE SUBJECT OF FISH DINNERS.
RIGHT!
RIGHT!
AND THE HOTEL WAS DESIGNED ACCORDING TO THE WHIMS OF THE COMPANY PRESIDENT.
THEY HAD A SYSTEM IN PLACE WHERE ONLY THOSE WHO ARRIVED UNDER THEIR OWN STRENGTH WOULD BE ALLOWED TO STAY.
WHOOOO
AAAAAH!
KYAAAA
SUDDEN GALE
MAKO GOT TO HIS ROOM WITH NO PROBLEM.
DAMMIT! I CAN'T MOVE!
IT'S SO FAR TO THE DOOR!
WHOOOOO
ITO-SAN!

I'd hate a hotel like that!!

HERE...
shwip
JUST GRAB ON TO THIS.
THEY SAY IT'S A SHOE-HORN.
WH- WHAT IS THAT?
A SHOE-HORN ?!
What part of that is a shoehorn?
THERE ARE NO SHOEHORNS THAT LOOK THAT WEIRD!
Wooden.
HOW ABOUT THIS?
A Back-scratcher.
FIND SOME-THING ELSE!!
BUT IN THE END, WE WERE BOTH BLOWN AWAY IN THE WIND.
WHOOO
AH!
← Caught up in it!
WE WERE BOTH BLOWN BACK INTO THE POOL... BACK TO THE START.
SLUMP
I SLEPT PRETTY WELL...
...BUT FOR SOME REASON MY BODY ACHES.
IT WAS A VERY TIRING DREAM.

YEAH, WELL... SORRY FOR THE WEIRD STORY.
ACTUALLY THE DREAM WENT ON LONGER.
IT HAD OTHER THINGS LIKE THE 306TH SUB-BASEMENT FLOOR.
IT'S VERY RARE FOR ME TO HAVE A DREAM OF THE CHARACTERS, AND MY MEMORY OF IT WAS REALLY VIVID, SO I DREW IT.
Dream Diary
WOULD YOU HAVE GRABBED THE LEG THAT MAKOTO SO CASUALLY BRANDISHED?
I used to write in this all the time before I got a continuing series. It was back then that I had the time.
I THINK THE W•J MANGA WOULD BE MORE FUN IF IT WAS LIKE MY DREAM.
I LOOK FORWARD TO MORE CHARACTER DREAMS!

2000. 4. 19. 絵夢羅。
E mura

Hakodate

[reference page 5] By treaty between the Shog and the U.S ambassador Townsend Harris, five ports in Japan were opened to foreign ships (after about 250 years of virtual isolation). One the most popular was Hakodate in southern Hokkaido. Hakodate is famous for its myriad of Victorian/Edwardian buildings and early signs o east/west interaction such as the Trappistine Convent (p. 12) and the Old Post Office, the Meijikan (p. 16).

Crystal-kan

[reference page 42] Situated in Otaru, a small port town west of Sapporo (called the "Venice of Japan" for its canal), the Crystal-kan is a museum of crystal and blown glass produced by the Kitaichi Glass Company.

Yukata

[reference page 30] A light cotton kimono which is usually worn in summer, but is often provided by hotels in lieu of a bathrobe.

Kamakura

[reference page 111] Snow huts called kamakura are a traditional part of winter, especially in northern Japan. And oden, skewered meat and vegetables in a soup, is a favorite when the weather gets cold.

Winter Holidays

[reference last two chapters] The winter holidays in Japan are reversed from Western tradition. In Japan, Christmas is a day for parties, dates, and celebrations. New Year's is the time for a quiet visit with family, for long-held traditions, and for religious observance.

New Year's is Japan's most important holiday with a huge number of important traditions. On New Year's the family plays games such as Iroha, a concentration-like card game. The Toshi-koshi soba ("passing-the-year noodles") are eaten. And the special present of money, Otoshi-dama, is given out to dependent children. People go to Shinto shrines, make an offering of money, and while wishing at the shrine's main building, they ring the bell so that the gods can hear them. On the shrine grounds, for a small fee people can pull a numbered stick from a box and receive a fortune according to the number. The fortune is then usually tied to the branch of a tree, making the tree look like it's in bloom even though it is January.

Hachifuku mochi

[reference page 166] "The Eight-fold Path to Happiness Rice Paste." Mochi ("rice paste") is a traditional food for New Year's, and there are several varieties including Chikara-mochi (power mochi), Ozoni (mochi soup), and Hachifuku mochi.

Chiba

[reference page 172] The prefecture just over the border of Tokyo's eastern city limits.

Kotatsu

[reference page 182] A special low table with quilted coverings over the top and a heater below for sitting and warming the legs during cold winter months.

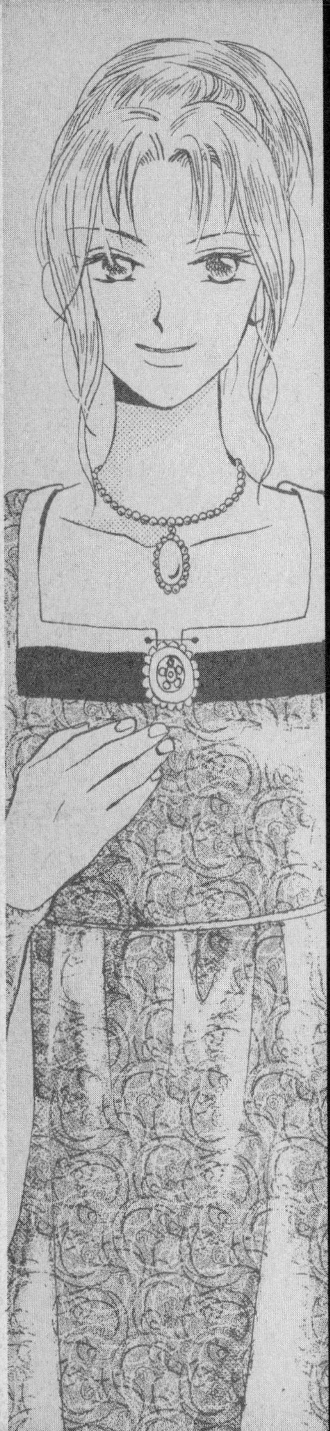

EDITOR'S RECOMMENDATIONS

If you enjoyed this volume of W Juliet then here's some more high school romance manga you might be interested in.

Doubt!!

Unremarkable Ai Maekawa navigates school life unnoticed...until one day when a spiteful classmate totally humiliates her in front of everyone. She decides to overhaul her image and enroll at a new high school where no one knows the old Ai. From the start, Ai is the target of romantic advances and jealous gossip--can a formerly invisible girl handle this avalanche of attention? And is Ai's identity as a loser really as far behind her as she'd hoped?

Cheeky Angel

Tough nine-year-old Megumi only ever wanted to be "the manliest man on Earth;" however, a hard-of-hearing genie misunderstood his wish and turned him into the "womanliest woman." Six years later, Megumi is the hottest girl in school, but has stayed true to his/her tough talkin', punk stompin' ways. . .

Here is Greenwood

If 15-year-old Kazuya Hasukawa's stomach wasn't perforated in a car accident, it would have been perforated by an ulcer! The woman he loves just married his older brother, and worse, he is bringing her home to live with them. Kazuya, forced out of the house, enters an exclusive all-male boarding school, Ryokuto Academy, more popularly known as "Greenwood." His roommate? Shun Kisaragi, the cutest girl in the guy's dorm.

COMPLETE OUR SURVEY AND LET US KNOW WHAT YOU THINK!

☐ Please do NOT send me information about VIZ products, news and events, special offers, or other information.

☐ Please do NOT send me information from VIZ's trusted business partners.

Name: ______________________________

Address: ______________________________

City: ____________ **State:** ______ **Zip:** ____________

E-mail: ______________________________

☐ **Male** ☐ **Female** **Date of Birth (mm/dd/yyyy):** ___/___/______ (**Under 13? Parental consent required**)

What race/ethnicity do you consider yourself? (please check one)

☐ Asian/Pacific Islander ☐ Black/African American ☐ Hispanic/Latino

☐ Native American/Alaskan Native ☐ White/Caucasian ☐ Other: ____________

What VIZ product did you purchase? (check all that apply and indicate title purchased)

☐ DVD/VHS ______________________________

☐ Graphic Novel ______________________________

☐ Magazines ______________________________

☐ Merchandise ______________________________

Reason for purchase: (check all that apply)

☐ Special offer ☐ Favorite title ☐ Gift

☐ Recommendation ☐ Other ____________

Where did you make your purchase? (please check one)

☐ Comic store ☐ Bookstore ☐ Mass/Grocery Store

☐ Newsstand ☐ Video/Video Game Store ☐ Other: ____________

☐ Online (site: ______________________)

What other VIZ properties have you purchased/own? ______________________________

____

How many anime and/or manga titles have you purchased in the last year? How many were VIZ titles? (please check one from each column)

ANIME	MANGA	VIZ
☐ None	☐ None	☐ None
☐ 1-4	☐ 1-4	☐ 1-4
☐ 5-10	☐ 5-10	☐ 5-10
☐ 11+	☐ 11+	☐ 11+

I find the pricing of VIZ products to be: (please check one)

☐ Cheap ☐ Reasonable ☐ Expensive

What genre of manga and anime would you like to see from VIZ? (please check two)

☐ Adventure ☐ Comic Strip ☐ Science Fiction ☐ Fighting

☐ Horror ☐ Romance ☐ Fantasy ☐ Sports

What do you think of VIZ's new look?

☐ Love It ☐ It's OK ☐ Hate It ☐ Didn't Notice ☐ No Opinion

Which do you prefer? (please check one)

☐ Reading right-to-left

☐ Reading left-to-right

Which do you prefer? (please check one)

☐ Sound effects in English

☐ Sound effects in Japanese with English captions

☐ Sound effects in Japanese only with a glossary at the back

DISCARD

THANK YOU! Please send the completed form to:

NJW Research
42 Catharine St.
Poughkeepsie, NY 12601

All information provided will be used for internal purposes only. We promise not to sell or otherwise divulge your information.